Y0-ABS-809

Burke's Politics

A Study in Whig Orthodoxy

Frederick A. Dreyer

Edmund Burke claimed to be a practical politician, rather than a theorist. Nevertheless, says the author, Burke held consistent political principles which form a coherent political theory. By examining concepts such as natural law, natural society, civil society, and history in Burke's speeches and writings, the author comes to some conclusions about Burke's political theory and its relation to commonly accepted eighteenth-century political doctrines. Succinct and balanced, this study will be of particular interest to political theorists and historians.

Frederick A. Dreyer is Associate Professor of History at the University of Western Ontario. He holds the Ph.D. degree from St. Andrews University, Scotland. He has contributed articles on Burke and British political history to various learned journals, including the Journal of Modern History *and the* English Historical Review.

Burke's Politics

A Study in Whig Orthodoxy

Frederick A. Dreyer

Wilfrid Laurier University Press

Canadian Cataloguing in Publication Data

Dreyer, Frederick A., 1932-
Burke's politics

Bibliography: p.
Includes index.

ISBN 0-88920-077-7

1. Burke, Edmund, 1729?-1797 – Political science.
2. Political science. I. Title.

JC176.B83D74 320.5'2 C79-094766-8

WILFRID LAURIER UNIVERSITY PRESS
Waterloo, Ontario, Canada N2L 3C5

79 80 81 82 4 3 2 1

For

My Mother

Contents

Acknowledgments

This book has its origins in an old argument with my colleague Roger Emerson over what it was that Burke actually said. I doubt whether I have convinced Roger that he is wrong and I am right, but I am sure that my work has gained much from the benefit of his opposition and criticism. I am indebted also to Ian Steele for his advice on imperial history and other matters and to John McLaughlin for his guidance on the French Revolution. My wife acted as final arbiter in all questions of style.

This book has been published with the help of a grant from the Social Science Federation of Canada, using funds provided by the Social Sciences and Humanities Research Council of Canada.

Chapter Two was first published in *Studies in Burke and His Time* 15 (Winter 1973-74) under the title, "Edmund Burke: The Philosopher in Action." It is reprinted here by permission of *Studies in Burke and His Time*.

One

Introduction

The student who tries to define Edmund Burke's political theory attempts something that Burke refused to do himself. He never wrote a political treatise and often affected to be a practical man who disliked speculation and who thought of politics in practical terms. "I do not pretend to be an antiquary, a lawyer, or qualified for the chair of professor in metaphysics," he told his constituents. "I never ventured to put your solid interests upon speculative grounds."[1] Defending the *Reflections,* he again rejected the role of a theorist: "I was throwing out reflexions upon a political event, and not reading a lecture upon theorism and principles of Government. How I should treat such a subject is not for me to say, for I never had that intention."[2] Burke's writings, nevertheless, are immensely rich in doctrine. And against his assertion that he was a simple, practical man, we can place the equally strong assertion that he was a man of consistent principle. In the closing paragraph of the *Reflections,* he claimed that he was a man "who in his last acts does not wish to belie the tenor of his life." The attack on the French Revolution he said came from one "who wishes to preserve

[1] Edmund Burke, *A Letter to... Sheriffs... of Bristol...,* in *The Writings and Speeches of Edmund Burke,* 12 vols. (Boston: Little, Brown & Co., 1901), 2: 222 (*The Writings and Speeches of Edmund Burke* is hereafter cited as *Works*).

[2] Edmund Burke, *The Correspondence of Edmund Burke,* ed. Thomas W. Copeland et al., 9 vols. to date (Cambridge: At the University Press; Chicago: University of Chicago Press, 1958-), 6: 304 (hereafter cited as *Correspondence*).

consistency, but who would preserve consistency by varying his means to secure the unity of his end."[3] He repeated this affirmation in the *Appeal*: ". . . if he could venture to value himself upon anything, it is on the virtue of consistency that he would value himself the most. Strip him of this, and you leave him naked indeed."[4]

This claim to a reputation for consistency does not prove that Burke deserved it. Some scepticism is no doubt justified. He spent most of his mature life as an active party politician. His great assertions of principle were made in the heat of party warfare. Even after he broke with his party over the French Revolution, he continued to write and speak like a politician. His controversial purpose always dominated his exposition of theory. Moreover, the assertions of principle that are scattered throughout his works are extremely difficult to fit together into a consistent and coherent theory of politics. On the interpretation put forward by Robert M. Hutchins, Burke often lapsed into profound contradictions: whether he acknowledged or denied the authority of natural right, social compact, or popular sovereignty depended upon the necessities of his case.[5] Hutchins' Burke is a "splendid rhetorician and advocate" but not "a seeker after truth" nor a philosopher.[6] This assessment has been repeated by Frank O'Gorman. On O'Gorman's account, Burke did not develop a systematic philosophy; it is vain to search for one in his writings; it is even useless to look for fundamental conceptions or key notions. If Burke is to be explained at all, it is not in terms of the ideas he held but in terms of the circumstances which elicited their statement.[7] The basic objection to this assessment is that it rests on dogmatic assumptions. Any proof of Burke's inconsistency is only as good as our interpretation of his statements. On a given reading of his statements a contradiction may be demonstrated. But what we may have proven is not Burke's lack of consistency but the falsity of our reading. To suppose, as O'Gorman does, that no reading of Burke will reveal a consistent pattern of thought may have a certain common-sense merit; it is not, however, a supposition that has been proven or can be proven. Admittedly, efforts to justify Burke as a theorist often explain his thought in terms of intellectual affiliations that are not compatible. John Morley's Burke had links with Montesquieu, Bentham, Coleridge, and Darwin.[8] Alfred Cobban's Burke is affiliated

[3] Burke, *Reflections on the Revolution in France* . . . , in *Works,* 3: 563.

[4] Burke, *An Appeal from the New to the Old Whigs* . . . , in *Works,* 4: 92.

[5] Robert M. Hutchins, "The Theory of the State: Edmund Burke," *Review of Politics* 5 (1943): 139-55.

[6] Robert M. Hutchins, "The Theory of Oligarchy: Edmund Burke," *Thomist* 5 (1943): 78.

[7] Frank O'Gorman, *Edmund Burke: His Political Philosophy* (London: George Allen & Unwin, 1973), pp. 13-14.

[8] John Morley, *Burke* (London: Macmillan & Co., 1907), pp. 70-73, 253, 314-15.

to Locke, to the Lake Poets, and to nineteenth-century nationalists.[9] Leo Strauss's Burke is part Thomist and part Hegelian.[10] For J. G. A. Pocock, Burke owed an intellectual debt to Matthew Hale and the seventeenth-century theorists of the common law. Yet Pocock also admits that there is a possible affiliation with natural law, romantic sensibility, and the theories of Hume and Montesquieu.[11] In Peter Stanlis' interpretation, Burke appears as a thinker who is both essentially Thomist and essentially eclectic.[12] It is possible that any one of these interpretations is true; yet each of them in different ways denies Burke's capacity for systematic and coherent thought. The issue that separates these authors from Hutchins is not whether Burke held a coherent theory but whether he held any theory with conviction.

If the question to be answered is what theory did Burke sincerely believe, we immediately run into immense problems of proof and interpretation. Whatever theory he formulated, it has to be deduced from party speeches and controversial pamphlets. There is no reason to think that Burke was consistently candid in his statements or that he adopted arguments simply because of their doctrinal authority. In the Regency crisis, he was presumably influenced by considerations that he did not introduce in debate. Burke asserted the rights of the Prince of Wales in terms of theory and constitutional law.[13] But upon the rights of the Prince depended the political fortunes of Burke and his party. If the Prince of Wales became regent with unfettered authority, Burke and his party would come into office. In the American Revolution, his defence of the colonists may have been dictated by private conviction; it may also have been dictated by party commitments. When we read Burke it is difficult to tell whether what we see is the statement of the party man or the confession of the formal philosopher. Like most public men he sometimes wrote in a representative capacity. Presumably, he was not free to write whatever he pleased when he compiled the reports for the committee on Indian affairs.[14] He wrote something

[9] Alfred Cobban, *Edmund Burke and the Revolt against the Eighteenth Century: A Study of the Political and Social Thinking of Burke, Wordsworth, Coleridge and Southey,* 2d ed. (London: George Allen & Unwin, 1960), pp. 37-38, 130, 244-45.

[10] Leo Strauss, *Natural Right and History* (Chicago: University of Chicago Press, 1953), pp. 296, 319.

[11] J. G. A. Pocock, "Burke and the Ancient Constitution: A Problem in the History of Ideas," *Historical Journal* 3 (1960): 143.

[12] Peter J. Stanlis, *Edmund Burke and the Natural Law* (Ann Arbor: University of Michigan Press, 1958), pp. 124, 249.

[13] Edmund Burke, *The Speeches of . . . Edmund Burke . . . ,* 4 vols. (London: Longman, Hurst, Rees, and Brown; and J. Ridgway, 1816), 3: 349-419 (hereafter cited as *Speeches*).

[14] Burke, *Ninth Report of the Select Committee . . . on the Affairs of India,* in *Works,* 8: 1-215; *Eleventh Report of the Select Committee . . . on the Affairs of India,* in *Works,* 8: 217-304.

that had to be adopted by the committee and issued under its authority. When he wrote *The Present Discontents* what he intended was a statement of the collective opinion of his party. Before publication the manuscript was sent to his friends for correction and endorsement; after publication, Burke spoke of the pamphlet as a statement of his party's creed.[15] In this instance it is impossible to tell whether Burke wrote what he privately believed or what he thought his friends were likely to accept. Scholars often assume that Burke spoke with a double voice. In one voice we hear the real philosopher who stated convictions and principles; in the other we hear merely the politician who said things for the convenience of debate. On the assumption of a double voice a great many things that Burke wrote may be dismissed from the interpretation of his theory. Morley ignored all of Burke's references to natural law; Strauss has discounted all of Burke's references to natural rights, the state of nature, and social contract.[16] Both authors supposed that Burke as a philosopher had rejected the Lockean theory of politics; both assumed presumably that Burke's Lockean statements did not count as evidence of his private theory. Any account of Burke's ideas that supposes he spoke with a double voice is objectionable for two reasons. First, there is no way of telling which voice is true and which is false. Secondly, the assumption puts the study of Burke's theory beyond the limits of proof and refutation. It becomes possible to argue that Burke was essentially Thomist or essentially Darwinian or essentially something else, and at the same time dismiss all evidence to the contrary as the insincerities of the politician. Whatever contradictions Burke's arguments may exhibit, they cannot be resolved on the assumption that he believed one half of the contradiction and not the other. In short we must treat the body of Burke's writings exactly as we would interpret the statements of a formal treatise. We have no choice but to assume that all of Burke's statements are equally credible or equally incredible as evidence of his theory.

Taking theory to mean a consistent pattern of argument, the following study will attempt to show that Burke did have a theory of politics. This theory does not display the rigour or the finish that we might expect to find in a formal treatise. Burke does on occasions change his mind and contradict himself. But in the main the principles he appealed to were remarkably coherent and persistent. To explain the contradictions that occur, it is not necessary to assume a profound confusion in the basic premises of his argument. He does not in fact shift back and forth from Thomism to Hegelianism or from Lockeanism to Romanticism. Nor does he contradict himself on the ques-

[15] Burke, *Thoughts on the Cause of the Present Discontents,* in *Works,* 1: 433-537; *Correspondence,* 2: 101, 108, 114, 118-21, 136, 139.

[16] Morley, *Burke*; Strauss, *Natural Right and History,* p. 296.

tions of natural rights, civil compact, or natural society. In all important respects Burke's theory is fully intelligible in terms of eighteenth-century political speculation. We do not need to suppose that he was either peculiarly old-fashioned or peculiarly original in his basic assumptions. Burke's theory was orthodox Whiggism in the sense that it was compatible with Lockean principles. Many of Burke's most important principles were in fact Lockean. In some respects Burke is more developed and richer than Locke, but in no respect did Burke adopt arguments which placed him in fundamental opposition to Locke. Burke did not rebel against the prevailing orthodoxy of his age; he argued about political questions in the very terms and on the same assumptions that his contemporaries did. The fact that he often differed from his contemporaries in the policies he supported or opposed does not prove that he was driven by a peculiar and eccentric theory of politics.

This analysis will attempt to unravel Burke's basic political assumptions; it does not, however, attempt to explain his political motives. No analysis of Burke's arguments can pretend to show why he supported the American Revolution, why he opposed the French, why he favoured Catholic emancipation, or why he adopted any cause that he did. A man's arguments in the end may be nothing more than pretexts that tell us very little about his motives. What an analysis of Burke's arguments can do, however, is to show us what the principles were that he understood and chose to assert. Many students of Burke are, no doubt, not content to know what it is that Burke literally said and argued. For them the basic question is not the letter of the word but the set of convictions and beliefs that inspired it. However, it is this preoccupation with his supposed beliefs and the neglect of his literal statement which have served more than anything else to confound the study of Burke's political thought. Once we ask what it is that Burke believed we pose a question which no evidence can conclusively answer. We can speculate endlessly about his conservatism, his Thomism, his organicism, and a host of other things without fear of refutation or hope of proof. But if we confine ourselves to the narrower question, if we simply ask what it was that he expressly argued, then we shall find that many of the principles which are attributed to Burke as beliefs are things that he never asserted and often denied.

Two

Natural Justice

Among all the different interpretations of Burke's theory which claim our attention, the most convincing is that which stresses his commitment to natural law. Like Locke, Burke acknowledged a natural moral law whose authority binds both the state and its citizens.[1] The development of this interpretation has been the work of many scholars,[2] not all of whom are in agreement on all points. Yet in its central and most important aspects the force of their common interpretation is difficult to resist. On many occasions Burke assumed the authority of natural law over the positive law of the state. He made explicit references to "the laws of Nature," to "the rights of Nature," and to the rules of "natural, immutable, and substantial justice."[3] He displayed a famil-

[1] Leo Strauss has disputed Locke's commitment to natural-law theory and finds in him a secret strain of Hobbesianism (Strauss, *Natural Right and History*, pp. 202-51). My own preference is for the standard reading of Locke. But what Locke privately meant does not concern us here. To show Burke's conformity to Locke, it is enough to understand the latter on the basis of his public statement and its vulgar interpretation.

[2] See among others: Strauss, *Natural Right and History*; Stanlis, *Edmund Burke and the Natural Law*; Francis P. Canavan, *The Political Reason of Edmund Burke* (Durham, N.C.: Duke University Press, 1960); Charles Parkin, *The Moral Basis of Burke's Political Thought* (Cambridge: At the University Press, 1956); Burleigh T. Wilkins, *The Problem of Burke's Political Philosophy* (Oxford: Clarendon Press, 1967).

[3] Burke, *A Letter . . . On the Penal Laws . . .*, in *Works*, 4: 236; *Fragments Of A Tract Relative To The Laws Against Popery In Ireland*, in *Works*, 6: 333 (hereafter cited as *Popery Laws*); *Speeches In The Impeachment of Warren Hastings . . . Speech in Opening*, in *Works*, 9: 340 (hereafter cited as *Impeachment Speech in Opening*).

iarity with formal and technical studies of natural-law theory and occasionally appealed to them in support of his arguments. In the *Popery Laws* and in the *Thoughts on Scarcity* he cited respectively Suarez and Pufendorf; in the impeachment of Warren Hastings and in *The Policy of the Allies* he made use of Vattel.[4] The references to Suarez and Pufendorf are somewhat slight and do not necessarily imply that he had a profound knowledge of either author. The debt to Vattel is more substantial. We might even suppose that it was Vattel's *Law of Nations* that supplied Burke with a natural-law argument to justify British interference in the French Revolution.[5]

The natural-law exposition of Burke's theory undoubtedly states something that is both persuasive and important. If it is at all proper to infer a theoretical system from Burke's political statements, natural-law doctrine must form a part and perhaps a very large part of that system. But because Burke *often* appealed to natural law as a basis of argument, we cannot suppose that he *always* appealed to it. Nor can we suppose because natural law served Burke in controversy that it also supplied him with a source of conviction and inspiration. There is no reason to presume that natural law necessarily motivated Burke or that every major argument he made must be translated into natural-law terms.[6] Peter Stanlis, one of the pioneers and leading exponents of the natural-law interpretation, appears to have made this presumption in his account of Burke's case against the expulsion and disqualification of John Wilkes by the House of Commons. Burke's defence of Wilkes in Stanlis' opinion supplies evidence of natural-law beliefs.[7] This judgment, however, is not confirmed by a close reading of Burke's speeches on the question. His case for Wilkes was stated entirely in jurisdictional terms. He made no crucial reference to natural law, nor did any of his arguments presuppose the authority of that law. What Burke disputed was not the competence of the sovereign power, but where that power was located under the British constitution. He admitted that the House of Commons might try its own members and expel them, but he denied that in passing judgment it had the power to invent new penalties, such

[4] Burke, *Popery Laws*, in *Works*, 6: 325; *Thoughts ... on Scarcity ...*, in *Works*, 5: 146; *Speeches in the Impeachment of Warren Hastings ... Speech in General Reply*, in *Works*, 11: 240 (hereafter cited as *Impeachment Speech in Reply*); *Remarks on the Policy of the Allies ...* , in *Works*, 4: 471-82.

[5] Burke, *The Policy of the Allies*, in *Works*, 4: 471-82.

[6] Cf. Strauss: "A single faith animated his actions in favor of the American colonists, in favor of the Irish Catholics, against Warren Hastings, and against the French Revolution" (Strauss, *Natural Right and History*, p. 295); cf. Stanlis: "In every important political problem he ever faced, in Irish, American, constitutional, economic, Indian, and French affairs, Burke *always* appealed to the Natural Law" (Stanlis, *Edmund Burke and the Natural Law*, p. 83).

[7] Stanlis, *Edmund Burke and the Natural Law*, p. 52.

as the incapacitation of Wilkes. The power of creating new penalties belonged to King, Lords, and Commons, acting together in Parliament; this power could not be usurped by any one of them acting by itself.[8] As far as it went the substance of Burke's argument was perfectly compatible with Hobbesian principles of government. This is not to suggest that Burke was a covert or latent Hobbesian. If his statements on Wilkes do not prove a philosophic commitment to natural-law principles, neither do they contradict such a commitment. But the point is that Burke did not always base his argument on an assertion of natural justice. In the Wilkes controversy the authority of natural law was ignored; in other controversies it was apparently denied. To demonstrate Burke's commitment to natural law, it is not enough merely to cite those statements where he obviously appealed to it. We must also account for those statements where he ignored the natural law or excluded it from consideration.

One of Burke's most explicit and thoroughgoing appeals to natural law appears in his early work on Irish anti-Catholic legislation, the *Popery Laws*. Burke never completed this work, nor was it published in his lifetime. But it does give us ample evidence of his private and youthful commitment to natural-law politics. The opening chapter consists of a technical summary of the penal laws; in this account there seems to be an implicit emphasis on those parts of the law that offended against natural justice. This emphasis is clearest in his treatment of the act of William III's reign which made it illegal for Catholic children to go abroad for education. The child who went abroad was presumably ignorant of the law and was presumably obeying the direction of his parents or guardians. Yet he, as well as his parents or guardians, was made liable to punishment. Moreover, the child could be convicted for an offence under the act without ever appearing for trial. His conviction followed automatically upon the trial and conviction of the people who sent him out of the country. Finally, even if on his return he could satisfy the court that the purpose of his trip was innocent and not contrary to the provisions of the act, the best that the court could do was to remit part, but only a part, of the penalty which it had imposed. On Burke's reading of the act, injustice was piled upon injustice. A child, who in nature was not free, was made criminally liable for the offences of his parents or guardians. He could be exposed to punishment without the opportunity to defend himself in court. And even if he was later proven innocent of any violation of the law, he must still suffer its penalties.[9]

[8] Burke, *Speeches,* 1: 73-79; *The Present Discontents,* in *Works,* 1: 503-504.

[9] Burke, *Popery Laws*, in *Works*, 6: 311-14. In 1782 he wrote that the "penalties and modes of inquisitions" prescribed by this act were "not fit to be mentioned to ears that are

In the following chapter Burke's references to natural law became clear and unmistakable. Hobbes was condemned by name. His principles were dismissed as being not only "unworthy of a philosopher, but of an illiterate peasant."[10] Over and over again the point was driven home that the positive law of the state must conform to the higher demands of justice. "All human laws are, properly speaking, only declaratory; they may alter the mode and application, but have no power over the substance of original justice."[11] If a positive law were to offend against justice in an important respect, then, "as this objection goes to the root and principle of the law, it renders it void in its obligatory quality on the mind. . . ."[12] Authors of unjust laws might allege that their victims had consented to their own oppression. Such a consent, Burke argued, would be "null and void"; "it would be made against the principle of a superior law, which it is not in the power of any community, or of the whole race of man, to alter. . . ." This superior law was, Burke continued, "the will of Him who gave us our nature, and in giving impressed an invariable law upon it."[13] In asserting man's obligations under the law of nature, Burke did not merely dwell upon the duties of obedience. He asserted also the rights of nature which its law implied. "Everybody is satisfied that a conservation and secure enjoyment of our natural rights is the great and ultimate purpose of civil society, and that therefore all forms whatsoever of government are only good as they are subservient to that purpose to which they are entirely subordinate."[14]

It would be a mistake, however, to force the natural-law interpretation of Burke's Irish politics much beyond his early years or much beyond the *Popery Laws*.[15] In the *Second Letter to Langrishe* of 1795 Burke's case for Catholic emancipation was stated entirely in prudential terms.[16] He not only failed to make a natural-law case for the Catholics but may even have forgotten that he had once done so in his youth. "In the Catholic question I considered only one point: Was it, at the time, and in the circumstances, a measure which tended to promote the concord of the citizens?"[17] The letter went on to press for concessions on the grounds that Catholic discontent could one day ripen into Jacobinism.[18] The absence of natural-law considerations is no less evi-

organized to the chaste sounds of equity and justice" (Burke, *Letter on the Penal Laws*, in *Works*, 4: 233-34).

[10] Burke, *Popery Laws*, in *Works*, 6: 322.

[11] Ibid., 323.

[12] Ibid., 319.

[13] Ibid., 321-22.

[14] Ibid., 333.

[15] Cf. Stanlis, *Edmund Burke and the Natural Law*, p. 46.

[16] Burke, *Second Letter to . . . Langrishe . . .* , in *Works*, 6: 375-84.

[17] Ibid., 378.

[18] Ibid., 379-80.

dent in Burke's first *Letter to Langrishe* of 1792.[19] Nowhere in this letter did Burke put forward a positive claim for the Catholics in terms of any right. Indeed, all claims of right were explicitly abandoned and excluded from consideration: "the whole question comes before Parliament as a matter for its prudence. I do not put the thing on a question of right. That discretion, which in judicature is well said by Lord Coke to be a crooked cord, in legislature is a golden rule."[20] There is no need, however, to suppose that Burke had changed his mind about the importance of natural justice. What had changed between the 1760s and the 1790s was not Burke's system of ethics but the character of the Irish question. In the 1760s the Irish Catholic could not buy a freehold; he could not educate his children; he could not freely practise his religion. By the 1790s substantial concessions had been made by the government. The question that remained was whether Catholics should be admitted to political rights on the same terms as Protestants: whether the Catholic should have the right to vote, to sit in Parliament, and to hold public office.[21] In the 1760s Burke was arguing about the rights which Catholics ought to enjoy under the government; in the 1790s he was arguing about their claims to be members of that government.[22]

Whatever natural rights Burke was disposed to acknowledge, it is clear from his other works that the claim to vote and to share in the government of the state was not one of them. He admitted that the right of man to govern himself was something he might possess in nature, but it was a right which he necessarily surrendered upon joining civil society; this natural right of self-government could not thereafter be invoked to justify a claim to civil authority. The sharing of civil authority within the state was a matter to be settled by convention on considerations of convenience. It was not a matter of natural right; "how can any man claim, under the conventions of civil society," Burke asked, "rights which do not so much as suppose its existence,—rights which are absolutely repugnant to it?"[23] Within the framework of contract and natural-law politics, the argument was solid and convinc-

[19] Burke, *A Letter to . . .Langrishe . . . on the Subject of the Roman Catholics of Ireland . . .*, in *Works*, 4: 241-306.

[20] Ibid., 292.

[21] Thomas H. D. Mahoney, *Edmund Burke and Ireland* (Cambridge, Mass.: Harvard University Press, 1960), pp. 325-42; William E. H. Lecky, *A History of Ireland in the Eighteenth Century*, new ed., 4 vols. (London: Longmans, Green & Co., 1892), 2: 213-17, 311-13; 3: 24-29.

[22] Burke himself recognized that the penal laws he had denounced in the 1760s were no longer the issue. "You know," he wrote in 1796, "that the far greater and the most oppressive part of those Laws has been repealed. The only remaining grievance which the Catholicks suffer from the *Law* consists in certain incapacities relative to *Franchises*" (Burke, *Correspondence*, 9: 124-25).

[23] Burke, *Reflections*, in *Works*, 3: 309-10.

ing. It had been forcefully stated in the *Reflections* in 1790 and again in 1791 in the *Appeal*.[24] In 1792, when he wrote the *Letter to Langrishe*, Burke could hardly turn Jacobin: he could not assert in Ireland a right which he had denied in France. His waiver of the claim of right in no sense threatened his consistency as a natural-law theorist. His manner of doing it, however, does reveal the influence of the politician and the practised debater. He did not give up the claim of right on the stated ground that no man could claim the vote as a natural right. None of his forceful anti-Jacobin reasons was brought forward; nothing was argued that would endanger the object of getting the Catholics the vote. Instead, the claim of right was given up on a pretext that was both trivial and flimsy. "Supplicants ought not to appear too much in the character of litigants." Subjects, he continued, should compliment their governors by appealing to their free discretion; governors should compliment their subjects by granting their reasonable wishes as if they were just demands; "in the fortunate conjunction of these mutual dispositions are laid the foundations of a happy and prosperous commonwealth."[25] Ostensibly, the claim of right was surrendered on a point of courtesy and not of logic. The casual reader might be excused if he read this passage and concluded that Burke possessed a very good case in right but was too gracious to assert it.

Burke's interest in the Irish question was largely personal; his interest in India sprang from official commitments, first as a member of the select committee on Indian affairs, secondly as one of the managers for the impeachment of Warren Hastings. In the impeachment speeches, as in the *Popery Laws*, Burke laid deliberate emphasis on natural justice. Surveying the general case against Hastings, he denied that actions which were crimes in Europe were not necessarily crimes in the Orient. Men who would justify Hastings on such considerations had, Burke argued, "formed a plan of *geographical morality*, by which the duties of men, in public and in private situations, are not to be governed by their relation to the great Governor of the Universe, or by their relation to mankind, but by climates, degrees of longitude, parallels, not of life, but of latitudes. . . ."[26] Nor could Hastings be defended on the pretext that he possessed an arbitrary power conferred upon him by the grant of his superiors or by the custom of the East. For Burke, no man could rightfully possess arbitrary power, nor could any man give it or receive it. "We are all born in subjection,—all born equally, high and low, governors and governed, in subjection to one great, immutable, pre-existent law. . . ."[27] Even if Hastings' authority

[24] Ibid.; Burke, *Appeal,* in *Works,* 4: 188; *Observations on the Conduct of the Minority* . . . , in *Works,* 5: 45-46.

[25] Burke, *Letter to Langrishe*, in *Works*, 4: 292.

[26] Burke, *Impeachment Speech in Opening*, in *Works*, 9: 447-48.

[27] Ibid., 455.

was not circumscribed by positive law, this did not cancel "the primeval, indefeasible, unalterable law of Nature and of nations." If this law of nature was violated, then its authority might be asserted by "downright revolt on the part of the subject by rebellion, divested of all its criminal qualities."[28]

The strong emphasis upon natural law, which was a conspicuous feature of the opening and closing speeches, was absent from the speech that introduced the sixth article of charge against Hastings. The sixth article accused Hastings of having taken bribes and presents contrary to law. Nowhere in the speech did Burke explicitly state that in accepting bribes Hastings had committed an offence against nature.[29] There may be many explanations for his neglect of natural law. First, the purpose of the speech was to introduce and explain the evidence which was to prove Hastings' crime. Caught up in the technicalities of his task, Burke may well have forgotten to make his usual appeal to natural law; or he may have felt that such an appeal would have been inappropriate to his purpose. It is also possible that Burke did not believe the acceptance of bribes to be a violation of the law of nature. The giving and taking of presents in nature he could have regarded as innocent acts which became crimes only when they offended against the obligations of positive duty. Finally, it is possible that Burke ignored natural law because it was not necessary for him to make use of it. Much of Hastings' conduct as it was described in the articles of charge was presumably immoral; how it offended against the positive law of the state was not made clear.[30] In the sixth article, however, Hastings was charged with the violation of an act of Parliament which had forbidden Indian officials to accept presents on any pretext.[31] Possessing for once a case in positive law, Burke may have felt less need to invoke the authority of Nature.

In the *Popery Laws* Burke had condemned positive law where it violated the law of nature. In the impeachment the authority of natural law was to be pushed one stage further. Burke condemned laws which although not contrary to natural justice were not clearly derived from

[28] Ibid., 459.

[29] Burke, *Speeches in the Impeachment of Warren Hastings . . . Speech on the Sixth Article of Charge*, in *Works*, 10: 147-451 (hereafter cited as *Impeachment Speech on the Sixth Article*).

[30] Burke, *Articles of Charge . . . against Warren Hastings . . . Presented to the House of Commons*, in *Works*, 8: 305-486; 9: 3-325. The charges that were finally preferred in the Lords were a slightly altered version of the charges that Burke had prepared for the consideration of the Commons (P. J. Marshall, *The Impeachment of Warren Hastings* [Oxford: Oxford University Press, 1965], pp. xiv-xv, 57). By professional standards the articles were obscure and imprecise: each was a separate essay detailing the misdeeds of Hastings; but only rarely and somewhat obliquely was Hastings accused of a specific breach of a specific law (William Holdsworth, *A History of English Law* [1938-66; reprint ed., London: Methuen & Co., Sweet and Maxwell, 1966], 11: 201-202).

[31] Burke, *Impeachment Speech on the Sixth Article*, in *Works*, 10: 325-26.

it: "you are not bound by any rules of evidence, or any other rules whatever," he told the Lords, "except those of natural, immutable, and substantial justice."[32] In their ordinary jurisdiction the Lords "moved within the narrow circle of municipal justice." Burke cautioned them against "forcing Nature into that municipal circle."[33] The offences that Hastings had committed were not transgressions of the mere form and letter of the law. They were crimes "against those eternal laws of justice." "His offences are, not in formal, technical language, but in reality, in substance and effect, *high* crimes and high misdemeanors."[34] In judging these crimes and in righting the wrongs suffered by the people of India, Burke told the Lords, "you will not suffer your proceedings to be squared by any rules but by their necessities, and by that law of a common nature which cements them to us and us to them."[35]

It was the common-law rules governing the admissibility of evidence to which Burke primarily objected. Much of the prosecution's case against Hastings relied upon evidence that could not be introduced if the ordinary rules were applied.[36] Burke had foreseen this danger and attempted to meet it in his opening speech:

> . . . I cannot shut my ears to the rumors which you all know to be disseminated abroad. The abusers of power may have a chance to cover themselves by those fences and intrenchments which were made to secure the liberties of the people against men of that very description. . . . God forbid it should be said, no nation is equal to the English in *substantial* violence and in *formal* justice. . . . An opinion has been insidiously circulated through this kingdom, and through foreign nations too, that, in order to cover our participation in guilt, and our common interest in the plunder of the East, we have invented a set of scholastic distinctions, abhorrent to the common sense and unpropitious to the common necessities of mankind, by which we are to deny ourselves the knowledge of what the rest of the world knows. . . .[37]

Part of Burke's objection to the rules of evidence turned upon a point of positive law. In administering their appeal jurisdiction, the Lords, he admitted, were bound to respect the rules of procedure which had been adopted by the lower courts. The impeachment of Hastings did not, however, come before them as a case in appeal. It was a matter for their original jurisdiction, and was to be tried not by the

[32] Burke, *Impeachment Speech in Opening*, in *Works*, 9: 340.

[33] Ibid., 343.

[34] Ibid., 338.

[35] Ibid., 344.

[36] James Mill, *The History of British India*, 9 vols. (London: J. Madden, 1840-48), 5: 122-256.

[37] Burke, *Impeachment Speech in Opening*, in *Works*, 9: 342-43. Burke later acknowledged that he had foreseen common-law objections to his evidence (Burke, *Report from the Committee . . . Appointed to Inspect the Lords' Journals . . .* , in *Works*, 11: 60; *Speeches*, 3: 535-36).

common law but by the law of Parliament. By referring questions of evidence to inferior judges and by adopting the procedures of inferior courts, the House of Lords had abdicated its responsibility and violated the constitution.[38] Thus far, Burke's objection was compatible with the Hobbesian doctrine of sovereignty. The House of Lords had assumed a discretion which it did not lawfully possess. It was not a sovereign authority and could not alter the law, any more than the House of Commons could alter the law in the Wilkes dispute.

Burke's protest against common-law rules of evidence, however, did not stop here. His second argument was grounded upon considerations of natural justice and to that extent attacked the application of those rules even in lower courts. In mere civil disputes over questions of property rights, Burke allowed to the courts and the legislature a wide degree of freedom to introduce artificial rules of evidence. Property was a right of nature; but most of its forms were inventions of civil society. Since those forms were artificial contrivances, artificial rules of evidence could be properly applied in their adjudication. Forms of property could be treated this way, "because their very essence, for the greater part, depends on the arbitrary conventions of men. Men act on them with all the power of a creator over his creature." In purely civil litigation men may introduce fictions and presumptions according to convenience; "and against those fictions, and against presumptions so created, they do and may reject all evidence." "Thus it is," Burke argued, "with things which owe their existence to men." But the exclusion of evidence, which was proper in the trial of civil disputes, was not proper in the trial of crimes. Here no evidence could be excluded which might influence the natural understanding of the court:

> . . . where the subject is of a physical nature, or of a moral nature, independent of their conventions, men have no other reasonable authority than to register and digest the results of experience and observation. Crimes are the actions of physical beings with an evil intention abusing their physical powers against justice and to the detriment of society: in this case fictions of law and artificial presumptions . . . have little or no place. The presumptions which belong to criminal cases are those natural and popular presumptions which are only observations turned into maxims. . . .[39]

Pleading what proved to be a bad case in positive law, Burke opposed to formal justice the higher claims of morality and natural understanding. It may be valid to cite his impeachment speeches as proof of his philosophic commitment to natural justice; but it should not be forgotten that this emphasis on natural justice was an essential part of the prosecution's case against Hastings. If he were to be tried by

[38] Burke, *Report from the Committee Appointed to Inspect the Lords' Journals*, in *Works*, 11: 49-59, 120-22.

[39] Ibid., 93-94.

the common law, there could be little chance of securing a conviction.[40] To win their case, the managers had to argue natural justice in one form or another. Burke was well aware of this. In his opening speech he warned the Lords against the influence of the common law and the influence of professional lawyers. He reminded the Lords that they were laymen and were bound to judge Hastings upon the principles of laymen. "It is by this tribunal that statesmen who abuse their powers are accused by statesmen and tried by statesmen, not upon the niceties of a narrow jurisprudence, but upon the enlarged and solid principles of state morality."[41] It was to be demonstrated over the next seven years that the Lords preferred to follow the lawyers and the common law; Burke's plea for the principles of state morality was ignored.[42] At the end of the trial Burke complained to Henry Grattan, "It is not always good to be tried by our Peers—for Nature in the choice of proper judges is more to be trusted than Magna Charta: But Nature is banishd by the formalities of Aristocracy. . . ."[43]

The trial of Hastings coincided with Burke's attack upon the principles and practices of the French Revolution. Here, his use of natural law was less conspicuous and less unequivocal than it had been in his Indian and early Irish works. Undeniably he did from time to time make explicit references to natural law. The French National Assembly was condemned for its confiscation of Church property. The Church's title to that property was grounded upon prescription; and prescription represented a "great fundamental part of natural law."[44] His case for allied intervention in France was based in part upon natural-law arguments taken from Vattel.[45] Furthermore, he urged the *émigrés*, in the event of a restoration, to distinguish between those rebels whose offences were merely political and civil, and those whose offences were crimes against the law of nature. The former, he argued, should be spared; the latter should be punished.[46] But in spite of this, his general commitment to natural-law politics seems to be contradicted by his denial of natural rights. In his speech on Unitarian relief all claims to natural rights were dismissed:

> What were the rights of man previous to his entering into a state of society? Whether they were paramount to, or inferior to social rights, he neither knew

[40] Marshall, *The Impeachment of Warren Hastings*, pp. 64-65; Holdsworth, *History of English Law*, 11: 202-203.

[41] Burke, *Impeachment Speech in Opening*, in *Works*, 9: 333.

[42] Mill, *History of British India*, 5: 122-256; Marshall, *The Impeachment of Warren Hastings*, pp. 64-65; Holdsworth, *History of English Law*, 11: 202-203.

[43] Burke, *Correspondence*, 8: 206.

[44] Burke, *Reflections*, in *Works*, 3: 433.

[45] Burke, *The Policy of the Allies*, in *Works*, 4: 471-82.

[46] Ibid., 463-64.

nor cared. Man he had found in society, and that man he looked at—he knew nothing of any other man—nor could he argue on any of his rights. As to abstract rights of all kinds, he thought they were incorporeal, and unfit for the body. They might be discussed in some other state; but they were totally unfit for this life, and consequently could not be fit for argument.[47]

In his speech on the Test and Corporation Acts, Burke assumed an almost Hobbesian transfer of natural rights to civil society.

Abstract principles of natural right had been long since given up for the advantage of having, what was much better, society, which substituted wisdom and justice, in the room of original right. It annihilated all those natural rights, and drew to its mass all the component parts of which those rights were made up.[48]

If Burke's remarks about the annihilation of natural rights are to be taken seriously then difficulties arise. First he appears to contradict the affirmation of natural rights which he had made in the *Popery Laws*.[49] Secondly, and perhaps more importantly, the significance of his natural-law professions is placed in question. It is impossible to conceive of a system of law which specifies duties and prohibitions but which does not imply rights. It is as if Burke were asking us to imagine that the law of nature as it works in society does not acknowledge a right to life but nevertheless commands us not to commit murder; or that it commands us not to steal but does not imply a right of property. Furthermore, if men may not plead their natural rights against the positive law of the state, then it is extremely difficult to understand in what sense the state is circumscribed by the law of nature. The same transaction which annihilates the rights of nature would appear by implication to annihilate the law of nature, which authorizes those rights. In short, if Burke's rejection of natural rights is total and unqualified, it would be extremely difficult to infer from his works a coherent political theory.

We need not, however, accept Burke's statement about the annihilation of rights in its simple and obvious sense. Usually his attacks upon natural-right theory were made in more guarded terms. In the *Reflections* he made a distinction between good and bad claims of right. "Far am I from denying in theory, full as far is my heart from withholding in practice . . . the *real* rights of men. In denying their false claims of right, I do not mean to injure those which are real, and are such as their pretended rights would totally destroy."[50] In a speech of 1792, he itemized a practical list of civil freedoms. It included rights of life,

[47] Burke, *Speeches*, 4: 51.
[48] Ibid., 3: 476.
[49] Burke, *Popery Laws*, in *Works*, 6: 333.
[50] Burke, *Reflections*, in *Works*, 3: 308.

property, and conscience. The Jacobin rights of man, he argued, went beyond this. They were "founded upon plausible deductions and metaphysical abstractions—true in some parts, and equally false in others."[51] The inference that natural-right theory was not entirely wrong and that the rights of nature were not completely superseded by civil authority was again prompted in his speech on the Traitorous Correspondence Bill in the following year. "Every kind of government . . . required that a man should surrender part of his natural rights to obtain those that belong to society; in a word, that he should forego part of his liberty for the security of the remainder."[52]

Burke made two suppositions that allowed him sometimes to assert and at other times to deny the authority of natural rights in civil society. The first supposition was not explicity stated, but it does seem to be implied by his speech on the Traitorous Correspondence Bill. Here he spoke of man making a partial surrender of his rights on joining civil society. He meant presumably that man transferred to the state his rights of government but retained his rights of life, property, and conscience; and these rights man could plead against the state if the necessity arose. On this supposition Burke could attack some claims of natural right without necessarily attacking all claims.

The second supposition was made more explicitly and persistently. It concerns not the number of rights which were transferred but the manner and the purpose of the transaction. Whether the transfer of rights was large or small, whether it was complete or partial, Burke often seems to assume that the citizen had made it in trust. "That he may secure some liberty, he makes a surrender in trust of the whole of it."[53] Now a conveyance of rights in trust is essentially a qualified transfer: the rights are vested in the trustee, but the trustee derives no benefit or advantage from his ownership; the benefits and advantages become the property of the equitable owner or beneficiary.[54] Burke must have imagined that Nature's court, like the English House of Lords, could hear appeals both in law and in equity. If equitable rights are not the same things as legal rights, they serve in Burke's theory, as they do in English jurisprudence, many of the same ends. In short, the equitable rights that arise from the trust permitted Burke to appeal from the positive law of

[51] Burke, *Speeches*, 4: 76.

[52] Ibid., 131.

[53] Burke, *Reflections*, in *Works*, 3: 310; *Speech . . . on . . . Fox's East India Bill*, in *Works*, 2: 439-40; *Speeches*, 2: 121, 257.

[54] Frederick W. Maitland, "Trust and Corporation," *Selected Essays*, ed. H. D. Hazeltine et al. (1936; reprint ed. Freeport, N.Y.: Books for Libraries Press, 1968), pp. 164-66, 170-73; George W. Keeton, *The Law of Trusts: A Statement of the Rules of Law and Equity Applicable to Trusts of Real and Personal Property*, 9th ed. (London: Pitman Publishing, 1971), pp. 207-11.

the state to some standard of natural justice. Supposing a large conversion of natural rights into equitable rights, it was still possible for Burke to argue that the authority of the state is limited. "We entertain a high opinion of the legislative authority"; he wrote in the *Reflections*, "but we have never dreamt that Parliaments had any right whatever to violate property, to over-rule prescription. . . ."[55] He could deny the survival of natural rights, but by sleight of hand he could quite consistently reassert the substance of those rights as benefits. "If civil society be made for the advantage of man," he wrote again in the *Reflections*, "all the advantages for which it is made become his right. It is an institution of beneficence; and law itself is only beneficence acting by a rule." The passage continued in a roundabout fashion to confirm the subject's usual rights to property and freedom of conscience. It concluded with the denial that the subject also possessed a right to share in the management of the state; "that I must deny to be amongst the direct original rights of man in civil society. . . . It is a thing to be settled by convention."[56] If we translate this passage into terms of equity, Burke may be understood to mean that the subject was the rightful owner of all the benefits which the trust could confer, but his beneficial rights alone did not authorize him either to be a trustee or to direct the administration of the trust.

In the matter of American taxation, natural justice and natural right were ostensibly excluded from consideration: "I am not here going into the distinctions of rights, nor attempting to mark their boundaries," Burke told the Commons in 1774. "I do not enter into these metaphysical distinctions; I hate the very sound of them."[57] This exclusion was repeated a year later in his *Speech on Conciliation*:

> . . . I am resolved this day to have nothing at all to do with the question of the right of taxation. . . . I put it totally out of the question. It is less than nothing in my consideration. . . . I do not examine whether the giving away of man's money be a power excepted and reserved out of the general trust of government, and how far all mankind, in all forms of polity, are entitled to an exercise of that right by the charter of Nature,—or whether, on the contrary, a right of taxation is necessarily involved in the general principle of legislation, and inseparable from the ordinary supreme power.[58]

Throughout the controversy Burke tended to argue against American taxation not in terms of natural right but in terms of expediency and prudence. Parliament may have possessed the authority to tax the

[55] Burke, *Reflections*, in *Works*, 3: 434.

[56] Ibid., 308-309.

[57] Burke, *Speech on American Taxation*, in *Works*, 2: 72-73.

[58] Burke, *Speech on Moving his Resolutions for Conciliation with the Colonies*, in *Works*, 2: 140.

colonies but the taxes it attempted to collect were offensive to the colonists and unprofitable to the state. "Your scheme yields no revenue; it yields nothing but discontent, disorder, disobedience. . . ."[59]

At first glance Burke's case against American taxation seems needlessly subtle and evasive. He had at his disposal after all a perfectly good natural-law argument. The Americans were not represented in Parliament; therefore, to force them to pay taxes constituted a violation of their property rights. This argument had been stated by Locke in section 140 of the *Second Treatise*;[60] it was widely used in the American controversy; and Burke was not unfamiliar with it. Given his general commitment to natural-law politics, Burke might well have used the argument himself. Yet he did not. Generally he either ignored or excluded it; less often he went out of his way to contradict it.[61] To explain this, we must remember that Burke was liable to a restraint that did not bind other critics of the tax policy. That restraint was the Declaratory Act of 1766 which had asserted the right of Parliament to legislate for the colonies "in all cases whatsoever."[62] The act had been sponsored by his friends in the Rockingham administration. His first votes as a new member of Parliament were given in its support.[63] Out of office Burke and the other members of the Rockingham party continued to defend the formal pretensions of the act. In his first piece of political writing, *A Short Account of a Late Short Administration*, Burke mentioned the act as one of his party's achievements in office.[64] In 1769 in his *Observations on a Late Publication*, he again applauded the act and stated specifically that Parliament possessed the right to tax the colonies.[65] In the *Speech on American Taxation* he asserted Parliament's right to tax and specified circumstances where that right might be properly exercised.[66] Burke was perfectly consistent in arguing that the mere possession of a right did not justify its use; but he was equally consistent in refusing to admit any argument that would compromise the right of taxation that the Declaratory Act had implied. He was in this sense as much wedded to the defence of abstract right as any man: and in the American crisis he adhered to the principle of the Declaratory Act with tenacity. The settlement he proposed in the spring of 1775

[59] Burke, *American Taxation*, in *Works*, 2: 75.

[60] John Locke, *The Second Treatise of Civil Government and a Letter Concerning Toleration*, ed. J. W. Gough, rev. ed. (Oxford: Basil Blackwell, 1948), p. 71.

[61] Burke, *Sheriffs of Bristol*, in *Works*, 2: 223; *Correspondence*, 3: 181.

[62] David C. Douglas et al., eds., *English Historical Documents* (London: Eyre and Spottiswoode, 1960-), 9: 695-96.

[63] Burke, *Sheriffs of Bristol*, in *Works*, 2: 235.

[64] Burke, *A Short Account of a Late Short Administration*, in *Works*, 1: 265.

[65] Burke, *Observations on a Late Publication, Intituled "The Present State of the Nation,"* in *Works*, 1: 385, 397.

[66] Burke, *Speech on American Taxation*, in *Works*, 2: 75-77.

in the *Speech on Conciliation* left the act unscathed. The Commons was urged to acknowledge the expediency of allowing the Americans to tax themselves; it was asked to resolve in favour of repealing the coercion acts; but it was not asked to repeal the Declaratory Act; nor did any of the resolutions which Burke moved contradict, even by implication, the formal right of taxation.[67] In the following autumn a second set of conciliation proposals was moved by Burke. On this occasion he urged the Commons to surrender the right of taxation. But this surrender was not urged at the expense of the Declaratory Act. Circumstances might require Parliament to give up an authority it undoubtedly possessed; circumstances did not require Parliament to admit that it had been morally or legally at fault in once having claimed those powers. "The repeal of a declaratory act," Burke argued, "was a thing impossible; for it was nothing less than to make the legislature accuse itself of uttering propositions that were false, and making claims that were groundless."[68] Because of his adherence to the Declaratory Act, Burke's range of argument in the American crisis was clearly circumscribed. Faced with the problem of defending the formal right of taxation, yet opposed to the exercise of that right, Burke was pretty well obliged to argue the issue in terms of expediency and prudence. Manifestly, he could not pretend that Parliament possessed the right to tax and that the colonists possessed the right to refuse whatever taxes they had not consented to.

It might be supposed that Burke's defence of the Declaratory Act and his opposition to the use of the powers which that act implied contradict his commitment to natural justice. Such a supposition would underestimate both his coherence and his adroitness. The powers he attributed to Parliament were, indeed, "boundless" and "unlimited."[69] But they were not the powers of a Leviathan state. Nor were the expedient considerations he urged against taxation merely those of a practical realist who was indifferent to all pretensions of right. In the *Speech on Conciliation* Burke had talked at length about the difficulties of raising a revenue from the proud slave-owners of Virginia and the stiff-necked dissenters of New England.[70] If the colonists had turned docile overnight, Burke's case against taxation would have been badly damaged; but it would not have been entirely destroyed. For in many of his arguments, he managed to insinuate the implication that the tax policy contradicted higher standards of justice. "It is not what a lawyer

[67] Burke, *Speech on Conciliation*, in *Works*, 2: 182-86.

[68] Burke, *Speeches*, 1: 354.

[69] Burke, *Speech on American Taxation*, in *Works*, 2: 76; *Sheriffs of Bristol*, in *Works*, 2: 223.

[70] Burke, *Speech on Conciliation*, in *Works*, 2: 120-25.

tells me I *may* do," Burke wrote, "but what humanity, reason, and justice tell me I ought to do."[71]

The device that allowed Burke to assign boundless powers to Parliament and at the same time question their use on the grounds of equity and justice was that of the trust, "that trust to which the order of Providence has called us."[72] Throughout his speeches and writings on taxation, the conception of the trust was both stated and implied. The power to tax was described in the *Observations on a Late Publication* as "a sacred trust in the hands of Great Britain." This power was to be used "not in the first instance for supply, but in the last exigence for control."[73] In a speech of 1770 perseverance in the tax policy was denounced as a betrayal of trust:

> The benefit of those that are governed is the ultimate end of all government, and not any supposed dignity of the governing power. It is very easy to discover what measures would now tend most to the general advantage both of the colonies and the mother country: and there can be no doubt but that these measures ought to be pursued, whatever mortification may ensue to the trustees of public power, who either weakly or wickedly have betrayed their charge.[74]

The trust was reaffirmed in the *Sheriffs of Bristol*:

> When I first came into a public trust, I found your Parliament in possession of an unlimited legislative power over the colonies. . . . I had, indeed, very earnest wishes to keep the whole body of this authority perfect and entire as I found it,—and to keep it so, not for our advantage solely, but principally for the sake of those on whose account all just authority exists: I mean the people to be governed.[75]

By implication, if not in so many words, the fiduciary relationship was assumed in his *Speech on American Taxation*. "I look . . . on the imperial rights of Great Britain, and the privileges which the colonists ought to enjoy under these rights, to be just the most reconcilable things in the world." It was Parliament's business to superintend the colonial legislatures "without annihilating any." These legislatures had to be subordinate to the Parliament of Great Britain, "else they can neither preserve mutual peace, nor hope for mutual justice, nor effectually afford mutual assistance." To allow Parliament "to answer all these ends of

[71] Ibid., 140-41. The other references to justice and equity are less emphatic. See Burke, *Observations on a Late Publication*, in *Works*, 1: 397; *Speech on American Taxation*, in *Works*, 2: 18, 24, 43, 53; *Speech on Conciliation*, in *Works*, 2: 154.

[72] Burke, *Speech on Conciliation*, in *Works*, 2: 181. Other statements that government is a trust are to be found in ibid., 102, 140; and Burke, *Sheriffs of Bristol*, in *Works*, 2: 227.

[73] Burke, *Observations on a Late Publication*, in *Works*, 1: 398.

[74] Burke, *Speeches*, 1: 20.

[75] Burke, *Sheriffs of Bristol*, in *Works*, 2: 223-24.

provident and beneficent superintendance, her powers must be boundless." In the event of war or a similar emergency, Burke went on, the purpose of this boundless power could justify taxation. "What! shall there be no reserved power in the empire, to supply a deficiency which may weaken, divide, and dissipate the whole?" If one or two colonies held back in the common effort, then Parliament might properly raise the taxes itself. "This is what I meant, when I have said, at various times, that I consider the power of taxing in Parliament as an instrument of empire, and not as a means of supply."[76] It was Parliament's duty, as a conscientious trustee, to maintain its authority. But this authority was to be maintained not for the sake of Parliament but for the sake of the colonist, who had a beneficial right to the maintenance and proper administration of that authority. Therefore, in justice the Declaratory Act had to be upheld. But the authority of the trust did not exist merely to be asserted and exercised without reference to the advantage of the beneficiary. Therefore, in justice the Stamp Act and the other revenue laws had to be repealed. If the Declaratory Act denied to Burke an argument in simple natural right, it did not deny to him an argument in equity.

When Burke wrote the *Appeal* in 1791, he defied his critics to show that there was any contradiction between the *Reflections* and his American speeches.

> On what part of his late publication, or on what expression that might have escaped him in that work, is any man authorized to charge Mr. Burke with a contradiction to the line of his conduct and to the current of his doctrines on the American war? The pamphlet is in the hands of his accusers: let them point out the passage, if they can.[77]

In this particular the challenge could be made with confidence. The defender of the Declaratory Act had never argued that the Americans possessed a natural right either to tax themselves or to govern themselves. Burke was not, therefore, under any obligation to admit to the Jacobin either a right of taxation or a right of government. Both the Jacobin and the American possessed rights as beneficiaries; neither possessed a right as trustee. If Burke's challenge is extended to the whole issue of natural justice, his general claim to consistency must be conceded. He asserted the superiority of natural justice over positive law on many occasions. This superiority was sometimes threatened, but he never denied natural justice in a clear and unambiguous statement. Considerations of natural right could be excluded or ignored: in his defence of Wilkes, in his case for the Catholic vote, and in his attack on Jacobin natural rights, Burke's argument was not based upon an ap-

[76] Burke, *Speech on American Taxation*, in *Works*, 2: 75-77.
[77] Burke, *Appeal* in *Works*, 4: 102-103.

peal to natural justice. But these exclusions of natural justice do not signify its denial. Here Burke argued on premises that neither asserted nor disputed the existence of natural justice. In the Jacobin controversy, Burke's argument in the end was not that there is no such thing as natural law or natural right; it was rather that the citizen could not base his claim to civil power on the authority of natural law or natural right. The jurisdiction of natural justice was restricted in the controversy; it was not totally denied. In the American controversy, Burke could exclude natural justice in determining whether Parliament could levy taxes. Here the positive and historic rights of Parliament were allowed to prevail over the natural property-rights of the subject. Yet when he came to consider the merit of the taxes that Parliament actually levied on the colonists, Burke reintroduced considerations of justice and equity. Of course, evidence of consistency does not prove philosophical inspiration. But whatever his motives may have been, Burke managed to preserve consistency in his appeal to natural justice. In his acknowledgement of the authority of historic and positive law, he did not abandon Locke for Hobbes.

Three

Natural Society

The belief that man had once lived in a pre-civil state of nature was a truism of eighteenth-century political speculation. It is often assumed that Burke denied this truism and acknowledged no important distinction between the state of nature and the state of civil society.[1] No doubt, Burke did reject state of nature theory in some of its forms. He never imagined that man could lead a solitary and unsocial existence. His natural society was not the natural society that had been supposed by Hobbes or Rousseau. Nor did Burke ever represent natural society as a utopia that civil man should strive to attain. But in another sense Burke stood squarely within the eighteenth-century tradition of natural-society politics. He assumed that civil society was an historical and artificial contrivance; he acknowledged the existence of a pre-civil state of nature as an historical fact; and he often argued that the regulations of natural society continued to govern man even after he had entered civil society.

The belief that Burke denied the possibility of pre-civil society probably springs from a mistaken reading of his *Vindication of Natural Society*.[2] In the *Vindication* Burke parodied Lord Bolingbroke's argument against revealed religion. If the mischief and misery it produced

[1] Stanlis, *Edmund Burke and the Natural Law*, pp. 76, 103, 127-28, 144, 164; C. P. Courtney, *Montesquieu and Burke* (London: Basil Blackwell, 1963), pp. 42-43; Carl B. Cone, "Burke and the European Social Order," *Thought* 39 (1964): 281; O'Gorman, *Edmund Burke: His Political Philosophy*, pp. 115-16.

[2] Cf. Stanlis, *Edmund Burke and the Natural Law*, p. 127.

were decisive against revealed religion, as Bolingbroke had argued, then on the same grounds Burke could demonstrate ironically that mischief and misery were decisive against the institutions of civil society. "Show me an absurdity in religion," Burke countered, "and I will undertake to show you a hundred for one in political laws and institutions. If you say that natural religion is a sufficient guide without the foreign aid of revelation, on what principle should political laws become necessary?"[3] It is not easy to get behind Burke's irony of statement in this work. But one thing is perfectly clear: nothing was written or argued in it that can be construed to deny the state of nature either as an hypothesis or as an historical fact. On the evidence of the *Vindication*, we can assume that Burke had no intention of returning to a state of nature. But the evidence does not prove that he ever denied the reality of it. Furthermore, we know that Burke's defence of revealed religion did not commit him to a denial of natural religion. It was not the truth or validity of natural religion that Burke disputed but its completeness and sufficiency. On one occasion he expounded natural religion himself.[4] He thought that man was a religious animal by virtue of reason and instinct.[5] He once spoke of natural religion as the beginning of holiness.[6] In a private letter, he professed respect for all religions, "even for those who have nothing better than mere human Reason, or the unregulated instincts of human Nature, for their Basis."[7] Because Burke defended the authority of revelation against the claims of natural religion, we cannot conclude that he condemned the latter as false. Similarly, because he defended the institutions of civil society, we should not conclude that he rejected all consideration of the state of nature.

Burke's clearest acknowledgment of the state of nature as an historical stage is to be found in the *Abridgment of English History*. Here he described the society of the primitive Saxons as a purely voluntary association. It lacked all civil or collective capacity. The Saxons on his account were ignorant of the principles of political authority. They knew nothing of deputation or representation. They had no authority which could act on behalf of the whole or bind the whole by its decisions. Common resolutions derived their moral force from the consent of everyone. Each man bound himself to his fellows to observe what all had resolved. Lacking the use of letters, Burke's Saxons could know nothing of law. Instead, they trusted to the force of custom. Their

[3] Burke, *A Vindication of Natural Society* . . . , in *Works*, 1: 64-65.

[4] Burke, *A Philosophical Enquiry into the Origins of our Ideas of the Sublime and Beautiful* . . . , in *Works*, 1: 126-27.

[5] Burke, *Reflections*, in *Works*, 3: 351.

[6] Burke, *Speech on a Bill for the Relief of Protestant Dissenters*, in *Works*, 7: 37.

[7] Burke, *Correspondence*, 4: 85.

"customs operate amongst them better than laws, because they became a sort of Nature both to the governors and the governed." The authority of the chieftains sprang from the force of influence and not from the formal rights of institution and delegation. "It was a species of arbitrary power, softened by the popularity from whence it arose. It came from popular opinion, and by popular opinion it was corrected." The chieftains were not legislators. If they acted as judges, it was in matters of small importance. And they acted by permission. The institution of civil society commenced with the ceremony of enlistment. When a young warrior received his weapons from the hands of a respected chief, the warrior bound himself in strictest dependence. Dependence was ratified by formal oath. "This was," Burke wrote, "the very first origin of civil, or rather, military government amongst the ancient people of Europe. . . ."[8]

A purely natural society might exist before the state was invented. It could also exist after the state was annihilated. In describing Massachusetts on the eve of the Revolution, what he described was a society that had abandoned its government and continued to cohere as a voluntary association. "Anarchy is found tolerable. A vast province has now subsisted, and subsisted in a considerable degree of health and vigor, for near a twelve month, without governor, without public council, without judges, without executive magistrates."[9] Burke did not rejoice in the anarchy he portrayed. In contrast to Paine, he did not imply that American anarchy demonstrated the superfluousness of government.[10] Burke shared the conventional belief that civil authority was a blessing. "I am much against any further experiments which tend to put to the proof any more of these allowed opinions which contribute so much to the public tranquility."[11] But in the end Burke was too good a citizen of the eighteenth century to deny either the reality or the importance of the state of nature.

Burke's natural society was not merely an event or stage that could be empirically discovered in history. It also figured as a necessary deduction from his conception of human nature. Man was a "gregarious animal."[12] He was never to be found in a state of isolation and independence. "It is not the condition of our nature. . . ."[13] Burke's idea of human nature displayed obvious affinities with the speculations of Adam Smith and the British Sentimentalists. Man discovered his moral

[8] Burke, *An Essay towards an Abridgment of the English History* . . ., in *Works*, 7: 291-94.

[9] Burke, *Speech on Conciliation*, in *Works*, 2: 129.

[10] Cf. Thomas Paine, *Rights of Man* . . . , *The Political Works of Thomas Paine* (New York: Liberal and Scientific Publishing House, 1878), pp. 113-14.

[11] Burke, *Speech on Conciliation*, in *Works*, 2: 129-30.

[12] Burke, *Correspondence*, 6: 80.

[13] Burke, *Three Letters . . . on the Proposals for Peace with the Regicide Directory of France*, in *Works*, 5: 321 (hereafter cited as *Regicide Peace*).

duties not through the exercise of reason but from the impulses of passion and instinct. These passions governed man's conduct and obliged him to fulfill a providential purpose. Burke espoused Sentimentalist doctrine in his youth;[14] he argued it with some formality in *The Sublime and Beautiful*;[15] and he continued to profess it throughout his life. He testified in the *Reflections* that "we . . . feel within us, and we cherish and cultivate, those inbred sentiments which are the faithful guardians, the active monitors of our duty, the true supporters of all liberal and manly morals." In the *Appeal* we find him writing in the same vein: "Dark and inscrutable are the ways by which we come into the world. The instincts which give rise to this mysterious process of Nature are not of our making. But out of physical causes, unknown to us, perhaps unknowable, arise moral duties, which, as we are able perfectly to comprehend, we are bound indispensably to perform."[16] To this extent, Burke's man was burdened both in civil and natural societies with social duties that owed little to his understanding or his consent. He was a member of society by virtue of his human nature. In the formal study of human nature that prefaced *The Sublime and Beautiful*, Burke identified three passions that were explicitly social in their effect and obligation. These passions were sympathy, imitation, and ambition.

Sympathy was the passion that compelled man to enter into the feelings of others. It made him suffer as they suffered and rejoice as they rejoiced. Nature had so constituted the mind, that man could feel the force of emotions that were given a fictitious representation in art and literature.[17] In his later works Burke often appealed to the force of human sympathy as a basis of argument. The case for virtual representation in part supposed the authority of the sympathetic passion. Because man could share in the emotions of others, virtual representation could be as effective and beneficial as formal representation.[18] He appealed to the authority of sympathy in the impeachment of Hastings. He argued that it was the duty of the managers to excite in the Lords a sympathy for the victims of Hastings' crimes. Providence had planted

[14] Edmund Burke, *A Notebook of Edmund Burke*, ed. H. V. F. Somerset (Cambridge: At the University Press, 1957), p. 71.

[15] Burke, *The Sublime and Beautiful*, in *Works*, 1: 117-19, 126-27. See Burke's letter to Adam Smith, September 10, 1759, written in praise of the *Theory of Moral Sentiments*: "I am not only pleased with the ingenuity of your Theory; I am convinced of its solidity and Truth; and I do not know that it ever cost me less trouble to admit so many things to which I had been a stranger before (Burke, *Correspondence*, 1: 129).

[16] Burke, *Reflections*, in *Works*, 3: 345; *Appeal*, in *Works*, 4: 166.

[17] Burke, *The Sublime and Beautiful*, in *Works*, 1: 117-22.

[18] Burke, *Letter to Langrishe*, in *Works*, 4: 293; *A Letter on the Affairs of Ireland*, in *Works*, 6: 418-19; *Speech on a Motion . . . for a Committee . . . into the State of the Representation . . .*, in *Works*, 7: 99 (hereafter cited as *Speech on Reform of Representation*).

in the breasts of men "generous and noble sympathies"; these were to be "the true guardians of the common rights of humanity."[19] The managers themselves had to feel the promptings of revenge as the Indians had felt them. To suppress these sympathetic feelings would be "base" and "degenerate." "This sympathetic revenge . . . is so far from being a vice, that it is the greatest of all possible virtues,—a virtue which the uncorrupted judgment of mankind has in all ages exalted to the rank of heroism."[20]

The argument that sympathy was a natural impulse and a guide to moral duty underlay Burke's attack on Richard Price in the *Reflections*. Here Burke condemned Price not only for bad political theory, but also for his failure to feel compassion for the misfortunes of the French royal family. Instead Price and his friends expressed feelings of exaltation and triumph. "This sort of people," Burke charged, "are so taken up with their theories about the rights of man, that they have totally forgot his nature. . . .They have perverted in themselves, and in those that attend to them, all the well-placed sympathies of the human breast."[21] Burke went on to recite the horrors of October 6, when the mob had seized the royal ramily and removed it from Versailles to Paris. He stated his recollection of the Queen as he had last seen her and contrasted her former happiness with her present misery.[22] Nothing in this recital was intended to prove the Queen's virtue and merits.[23] Burke's purpose rather was to state the dramatic circumstances that ought to have aroused the compassion of natural man. "Oh! what a revolution! and what an heart must I have, to contemplate without emotion that elevation and that fall!"[24] Why, Burke asked, did he feel so differently from Price and his friends? "For this plain reason," he answered, "Because it is *natural* I should; because we are so made as to be affected at such spectacles with melancholy sentiments . . . because in events like these our passions instruct our reason. . . ."[25] The principle that sustained this attack on Price was not the invention of the moment nor the consequence of rhapsodic enthusiasm. In its essentials Burke had committed himself to this argument when he wrote *The Sublime and Beautiful*. Natural man ought to feel sympathy for his fellows; if the impulse of sympathy is denied in circumstances that ought to arouse it, then the offender yields to perversion; he cuts himself off from the bonds of natural society. On

[19] Burke, *Impeachment Speech on the Sixth Article*, in *Works*, 10: 311.

[20] Burke, *Impeachment Speech in Reply*, in *Works*, 11: 179.

[21] Burke, *Reflections*, in *Works*, 3: 316.

[22] Ibid., 325-31.

[23] Burke, *Correspondence*, 6: 89-91.

[24] Burke, *Reflections*, 3: 331.

[25] Ibid., 337.

this assumption Price's exultation could be condemned as "the degenerate choice of a vitiated mind."[26]

The second of the social passions was imitation. This, Burke explained in *The Sublime and Beautiful*, compelled man to copy what other men did. It was on the impulse of imitation that men acquired knowledge. Thus imitation could be said to form "our manners, our opinions, our lives." Moreover imitation supplied one of the strongest ties of social union: " . . . it is a species of mutual compliance, which all men yield to each other, without constraint to themselves, and which is extremely flattering to all."[27] That Burke assumed the operation of this passion was of extreme importance for his social theory. Imitation, however, did not figure very explicitly in his controversial writings. Perhaps the only occasion where it provided Burke with a basis of argument is to be found in the *Regicide Peace*. Here he condemned the prospect of a peace-treaty with the French Republic. Peace and friendship, he argued, could not be assured by the artificial bonds of formal treaty. "Men are not tied to one another by papers and seals." Friendship between nations like friendship between men was to be secured "by resemblances, by conformities, by sympathies." "Nothing is so strong a tie of amity between nation and nation," he went on, "as correspondence in laws, customs, manners, and habits of life. They have more than the force of treaties in themselves. They are obligations written in the heart. They approximate men to men without their knowledge, and sometimes against their intentions."[28] The natural bond which tied man to man had been deliberately severed by the French. They had willfully departed from "every one of the ideas and usages, religious, legal, moral, or social, of this civilized world." Their eccentricity was "a violent breach in the community of Europe"; it was "a schism with the whole universe."[29] The French presumably had denied the impulse of imitation and disavowed any link with the society of the human race.

The third of Burke's social passions was ambition. "God has planted in man a sense of ambition, and a satisfaction arising from the contemplation of his excelling his fellows in something deemed valuable amongst them." Man might derive a natural satisfaction from almost any peculiarity in his character or in his circumstances. "Whatever, either on good or upon bad grounds, tends to raise a man in his own opinion, produces a sort of swelling and triumph, that is extremely grateful to the human mind. . . ."[30] The claims of this passion were

[26] Ibid., 320.

[27] Burke, *The Sublime and Beautiful*, in *Works*, 1: 122.

[28] Burke, *Regicide Peace*, in *Works*, 5: 317-18.

[29] Ibid., 320.

[30] Burke, *The Sublime and Beautiful*, in *Works*, 1: 124.

acknowledged by men because they were also moved by an impulse that made them feel astonishment and admiration.[31] On the basis of these reciprocal impulses Burke could proceed to argue that aristocracy was a natural institution. Some men led and others followed not because of formal arrangements and obligations, but from the natural operation of men's passions. Burke's first statement of this theory was made in the *Abridgment of English History*. Describing Saxon society, he wrote:

> ... the whole of their government ... [depended] for the most part upon two principles in our nature,—ambition, that makes one man desirous, at any hazard or expense, of taking the lead amongst others,—and admiration, which makes others equally desirous of following him, from the mere pleasure of admiration, and a sort of secondary ambition, one of the most universal passions among men. These two principles, strong, both of them, in our nature, create a voluntary inequality and dependence.[32]

It is important to understand that the aristocracy whose claims Burke asserted was in no sense a formal body instituted by the state. Burke's natural aristocrat might be a person without distinctive civil rank. In the *Appeal* his definition of the natural aristocracy included merchants, lawyers, clergymen, intellectuals, and men of good education and breeding.[33] The natural representatives of the British people, as Burke described them in the *Regicide Peace*, numbered about four hundred thousand men. This number included "those of adult age, not declining in life, of tolerable leisure ... of some means of information ... and who are above menial dependence." What he had in mind was obviously not the British nobility; nor was it the British electorate. Curiously enough, it was not even a collection of wise and virtuous men. He estimated that one-fifth of the natural representatives were Jacobins, men who were "utterly incapable of amendment" and who ought to be "objects of eternal vigilence."[34] Burke's aristocrat was simply a man whose circumstances and attainments allowed him to influence others and figure as their representative. He was an aristocrat by virtue of his natural qualities that entitled him to command deference and respect. "Give once a certain constitution of things," Burke argued in the *Appeal*, "which produces a variety of conditions and circumstances in a state, and there is in Nature and reason a principle which ... postpones, not the interest, but the judgment, of those who are *numero plures*, to those who are *virtute et honore majores*."[35] For Burke there could be no kind of artificial privilege that might transform the Irish Protestants into a natural aristocracy. "The Protes-

[31] Ibid., 130.
[32] Burke, *Abridgment of English History*, in *Works*, 7: 295.
[33] Burke, *Appeal*, in *Works*, 4: 175.
[34] Burke, *Regicide Peace*, in *Works*, 5: 284-85.
[35] Burke, *Appeal*, in *Works*, 4: 174.

tants of Ireland . . . are *too numerous* to answer the ends and purposes of *an aristocracy*. Admiration, that first source of obedience, can be only the claim or the imposture of the few." Whatever pre-eminence the Irish Protestant enjoyed was purely artificial and contrived: it was the supremacy of one plebeian over another and not the supremacy of the true aristocrat.[36]

Burke's first statement of the claims of the natural aristocracy is found in *The Present Discontents*. The purpose of this pamphlet was to condemn the King for the misuse of public patronage. On Burke's account George III's predecessors had appointed ministers who were men "of great natural interest or great acquired consideration." The old practice had a double advantage. It attached the adherents of the natural aristocrats to the government; it gave to the people an assurance of their own importance in the conduct of affairs. But the advantage that made such appointments desirable on public grounds made them offensive to the court of George III. "It is the nature of despotism to abhor power held by any means but its own momentary pleasure; and to annihilate all intermediate situations between boundless strength on its own part, and total debility on the part of the people."[37] On his accession, George III dismissed the natural aristocrats from office and appointed men who lacked an independent standing. "The lead," Burke said, "was to be given to men of no sort of consideration or credit in the country. This want of natural importance was to be their very title to delegated power." Parliament was drilled in the doctrine that the King possessed the right to appoint to office whomever he pleased. "Points of honor and precedence were no more to be regarded in Parliamentary decorum than in a Turkish army. It was to be avowed, as a constitutional maxim, that the king might appoint one of his footmen, or one of your footmen for minister; and that he ought to be, and that he would be, as well followed as the first name for rank or wisdom in the nation."[38] In his attack on George III, Burke had foreshadowed the argument that he was to make against the French revolutionaries in the *Reflections*. For the same reasons that it was absurd to make a footman minister, it was absurd to place the common people of France in stations of authority. "Believe me," Burke wrote in the *Reflections*, "those who attempt to level never equalize. In all societies consisting of various descriptions of citizens, some description must be uppermost. The levellers, therefore, only change and pervert the natural order of things." To put tailors and carpenters into office was "the worst of usurpations, an usurpation on the prerogatives of Nature." Men of menial occupations should not be oppressed by the

[36] Burke, *Letter to Langrishe*, in *Works*, 4:251-52.

[37] Burke, *The Present Discontents*, in *Works*, 1: 445-46.

[38] Ibid., 448-49.

state. But, Burke concluded, " . . . the state suffers oppression, if such as they, either individually or collectively, are permitted to rule. In this you think you are combating prejudice, but you are at war with Nature."[39]

Admittedly, Burke's argument in *The Present Discontents* displays a democratic purpose that is absent in the *Reflections*. In the *Reflections* the claims of the natural aristocracy were asserted against the artificial pretensions of the people. In *The Present Discontents*, the claims of the aristocracy were asserted on behalf of the people against the artificial rights of the King. *The Present Discontents* represented the aristocracy almost as agents of the public will. They were the representatives of the people whose deference and respect they were presumed to deserve. In this context the greatness and influence of a peer arose from the favour of the people; to place the peer in office was to give the people a pledge of their own importance.[40] The natural authority of an aristocracy was argued for different purposes in the two works. But the differences of statement and application do not prove a contradiction in Burke's underlying assumptions. In both cases he attacked a purely formal and artificial distribution of civil authority. He denied that this distribution could be justified either by the legal rights of the King or by the speculative rights of man. In both cases the artificial arrangement was condemned on the grounds that it could not be reconciled to the necessities of human nature or to the realities of natural society. In both cases he assumed the authority of an aristocratic order in nature that man could not pervert by the contrivances of artificial policy.

Towards the end of his life Burke can be found accounting for the authority of the state in largely naturalist terms. This tendency is most evident in his anti-Jacobin works. "We preserve," he wrote in the *Reflections*,

> the whole of our feelings still native and entire, unsophisticated by pedantry and infidelity. We have real hearts of flesh and blood beating in our bosoms. We fear God; we look up with awe to kings, with affection to Parliaments, with duty to magistrates, with reverence to priests, and with respect to nobility. Why? Because, when such ideas are brought before our minds, it is *natural* to be so affected; because all other feelings are false and spurious.[41]

In the *Regicide Peace* the same emphasis re-appears. "The body politic of France existed in the majesty of its throne, in the dignity of its nobility, in the honor of its gentry, in the sanctity of its clergy, in the reverence of its magistracy. . . . All these particular *moleculae* united form the great mass of what is truly the body politic in all countries."[42]

[39] Burke, *Reflections*, in *Works*, 3: 295-96.

[40] Burke, *The Present Discontents*, in *Works*, 1: 458, 473.

[41] Burke, *The Reflections*, in *Works*, 3: 345-46.

[42] Burke, *Regicide Peace*, in *Works*, 5: 326.

In both statements Burke ignored the formal basis of civil duty. The citizen was presumed to obey the state because his natural feelings prompted him to respect the qualities that its officials and dignitaries possessed. Whatever the artificial source of civil duty may have been, the citizen owed to the government a measure of instinctive obedience. To this extent Burke's state can be explained in terms that are appropriate to a natural and voluntary community.

The strongest evidence for a completely naturalist interpretation of Burke's state is to be found in the *Appeal*. Here he argued that the primacy of a natural aristocracy represented a condition for civil association. If this condition were violated, then the community failed and forfeited all rights to be regarded as a civil society. The existence of a society supposed an "habitual social discipline." Under this discipline the wise and the rich guided the ignorant and the poor. "When the multitude are not under this discipline, they can scarcely be said to be in civil society." A true natural aristocracy could not be separated from the state. "It is an essential integrant part of any large body rightly constituted." The creation of this aristocracy was not simply the institution of civil policy. "The state of civil society which necessarily generates this aristocracy is a state of nature." The aristocrats "form in Nature, as she operates in the common modification of society, the leading, guiding, and governing part." To treat them as the equals of their inferiors in the natural order of society was "a horrible usurpation." The argument continued:

> When great multitudes act together, under that discipline of Nature, I recognize the PEOPLE. I acknowledge something that perhaps equals, and ought always to guide, the sovereignty of convention. In all things the voice of this grand chorus of national harmony ought to have a mighty and decisive influence. But when you disturb this harmony,—when you break up this beautiful order, this array of truth and Nature, as well as of habit and prejudice,—when you separate the common sort of men from their proper chieftains, so as to form them into an adverse army,—I no longer know that venerable object called the people in such a disbanded race of deserters and vagabonds. . . . The mind owes to them no sort of submission. They are, as they have always been reputed, rebels. They may lawfully be fought with and brought under, whenever an advantage offers.[43]

If Burke assumed in this passage a purely naturalist theory of civil society, the assumption was not explicitly stated. He did not write, as it is sometimes thought, that the state of civil society is a state of nature.[44]

[43] Burke, *Appeal*, in *Works*, 4: 174-77.

[44] Cf. Stanlis, *Edmund Burke and the Natural Law*, pp. 131, 206; Parkin, *The Moral Basis of Burke's Political Thought*, p. 22; R. R. Fennessy, *Burke, Paine and the Rights of Man* (The Hague: Martinus Nijhoff, 1963), p. 71.

The sentence that reads, "The state of civil society which necessarily generates this aristocracy is a state of Nature . . . ,"[45] can bear only one interpretation. This is that the formal institution of an aristocracy conforms to the realities of human nature and does not violate what Burke calls "the natural order of life."[46] Indeed, "the natural order of life" is offended against, if men in their artificial contrivances attempt to destroy the aristocracy that nature generates. The sentence does not justify the construction that there is no difference between a state of nature and a state of civil society. Throughout the passage Burke kept up a formal distinction between the two "states." He acknowledged a difference between the "discipline of Nature" and "the sovereignty of convention." The former, he argued, ought to guide the latter.[47] We cannot take Burke to mean that the former was identical with the latter. The naturalist interpretation of civil society is not suggested by anything that Burke explicitly asserted in this passage. It is suggested, rather, by the way the argument developed and the conclusions he reached. He started his defence of the natural aristocracy on considerations of utility. Presumably, it was good policy for a people to consult the natural order of life in settling their purely civil institutions. The recognition of aristocratic leadership was of benefit to the people.[48] But very quickly Burke shifts his ground from a consideration of utility to a consideration of legitimacy. Once the natural eminence of the aristocrat is denied, the artificial society of the people forfeits its civil cohesion and its title to civil authority. On Burke's account the violation of the natural order terminates the existence of the civil order. The people became deserters and vagabonds; the mind owed them no sort of submission; they could lawfully be fought with and brought under whenever an advantage offered.[49] It was one thing for Burke to assert the realities of natural society as a consideration of convenience and prudence. It was quite another thing for him to conclude that the destruction of the natural order destroyed the legitimacy of the state. This conclusion requires us to suppose that civil society derived its rightful authority not from the sovereignty of convention but from the discipline of nature.

There is no reason to think, however, that Burke acknowledged the premises to which his conclusion committed him. He might write as if the dissolution of the natural society destroyed the authority of the state; he could also write as if the dissolution of the state destroyed the natural society. In the *Appeal* these two arguments were stated consecu-

[45] Burke, *Appeal*, in *Works*, 4: 175.
[46] Ibid., 177.
[47] Ibid., 176.
[48] Ibid., 174.
[49] Ibid., 176.

tively. And the latter argument appears to be more explicit and deliberate of the two.

> In a state of *rude* Nature there is no such thing as a people. A number of men in themselves have no collective capacity. The idea of a people is the idea of a corporation. It is wholly artificial, and made, like all other legal fictions, by common agreement. . . . When men . . . break up the original compact or agreement which gives its corporate form and capacity to a state, they are no longer a people,—they have no longer a corporate existence,—they have no longer a legal coactive force to bind within, nor a claim to be recognized abroad. They are a number of vague, loose individuals, and nothing more.[50]

On the evidence of this statement, a natural society, however disciplined and cohesive it may be, does not constitute a state. If Burke did think of the state as an entirely natural institution, it was not an idea that he argued with explicitness and consistency. Burke in the *Appeal* had assumed two essentially different conceptions of society. In one conception it was a natural association that derived its cohesion from the force of human passions; in the other it was a juridical association that derived its authority from the obligations its members had formally assumed. The two conceptions of society did not contradict each other. It is conceivable that the social ties of civil men are in some respects artificial and in other respects natural. On prudential grounds it is conceivable that the governors of artificial society should be obliged to heed the natural order of life. Burke undoubtedly mis-stated his case when he tried to argue that the society of artifice and the society of nature were related jurisdictions. The violation of the natural order cannot dissolve the artificial society; nor can the violation of the artificial society dissolve the natural. Here he lapsed into a *non sequitur*. But in the end it is more significant that Burke assumed a distinction between the two conceptions of society than that he once obscured it in debate.

Burke's appeal to the discipline of nature is not something that finds a conspicuous counterpart in Locke. In the *Second Treatise*, Locke had argued his case in largely juridical and legitimist terms; he paid little or no attention either to the passions of man or to the particulars of the natural social order. Burke's emphasis on natural society clearly owed more to the speculations of his contemporaries than it did to Locke. Burke began to write and think more than two generations after Locke's death; Burke's appeal to a natural social order in its spirit and emphasis is much closer to the *Wealth of Nations* than to the *Second Treatise*. Yet this appeal should not be read as a rejection of Locke or even as a significant departure from the framework of Lockean theory. For the notion that man is by inclination a member of natural society

[50] Ibid., 169-70.

and by contrivance a member of civil society is at bottom a Lockean notion. It is crucial to the Lockean theory of politics. Locke had little choice but to assume that society was in some respects artificial and in other respects natural. If he had supposed that society was only artificial, then he lost his case against Hobbes. If he had supposed that it was only natural, then he lost it against Filmer. The exploration of natural society and the study of its significance for civil government were tasks that Locke had bequeathed to the eighteenth century. They were tasks that Burke and his contemporaries could undertake without forfeiting their Lockean credentials.

Four

Civil Society

Burke's conception of civil society is probably the most puzzling feature of his political theory. Sometimes his state appears to be a superhuman authority to which man owes an involuntary obedience. At other times it is a human institution that man has made and chosen to obey. If this is an inconsistency in his theory, it is not one that can be explained on the assumption that he thought different things at different times. For the "contradiction" can appear within the context of a single work. At one point in the *Reflections* he wrote of God as the "Institutor and Author and Protector of civil society." At another point he described government as "a contrivance of human wisdom to provide for human *wants*."[1] In *The Present Discontents* the "contradiction" was stated within the compass of a single sentence: ". . . government certainly is an institution of divine authority, yet its forms, and the persons who administer it, all originate from the people."[2] It is possible, however, to study Burke's state without first determining its pedigree. Whether the state was made by God or by man, Burke thought of it as a legal institution. Sometimes he conceived of it as an agency, very often as a trust, and sometimes as a corporation or body-politic. The first question we must ask ourselves in reading Burke is not who authorized his state but what its legal capacity was.

Of the three identities that Burke gave to the state, that of agency was the least explicit and least fully developed. The evidence for its

[1] Burke, *Reflections,* in *Works,* 3: 361, 310.

[2] Burke, *The Present Discontents,* in *Works,* 1: 492.

adoption is mainly confined to the *Popery Laws*. Here government tended to figure as an attorney. He described the King as the "national procurator."[3] The authority of the people approximated the authority of a principal. Government had the power to legislate positive law; but the people had merely given up their judgment and not their right. "In all forms of government," Burke contended, "the people is the true legislator. . . ." Government was only "the immediate and instrumental cause of the law"; the "remote and efficient cause" was the consent of the people. This consent might be either actual or implied; but in one form or another, it was "absolutely essential" to the validity of a law. Whenever a law benefited the people their ratifying consent could be presumed. No consent could be presumed when a law injured them: ". . .such a constitution cannot in propriety be a law at all."[4] The notion that the validity of a law supposed the consent of the people in any form is not characteristic of Burke's later thought. Holding to this conception of the state, Burke would have found it very difficult either to justify the Declaratory Act or to attack the Jacobins.

In another sense, however, the conception of the state as agent was to prove more durable. He assumed that the state might commit the people to binding contracts. The contract which he defended in the *Popery Laws* was the Treaty of Limerick of 1691. In this treaty William III had guaranteed to the Irish Jacobites that Catholic rights would be respected. In making this guarantee, Burke argued, William represented "the whole contracting capacity of the nation." There was in the state no "dormant" or "irresistible" power that could absolve the people from the obligation that William had assumed on their behalf. "The compact of the king acting constitutionally was the compact of the nation." On the assumption that the Treaty of Limerick was binding upon the nation, Burke could dispute the validity of the penal laws that Parliament had subsequently legislated.[5]

The idea that the state could negotiate binding contracts never entirely vanished from Burke's theory. He acknowledged this capacity in the debate over Fox's India bill.[6] Although none too explicitly, it was assumed in his efforts to obtain a treaty for the American rebels.[7] Yet on these occasions Burke did not assert the authority of public contract with the same absoluteness that he exhibited in his defence of the Treaty of Limerick. The state of Burke's later conception possessed rights and duties that it could not alienate by contract. The evidence for

[3] Burke, *Popery Laws*, in *Works*, 6: 350.

[4] Ibid., 320-21.

[5] Ibid., 349-50.

[6] Burke, *Speech on Fox's East India Bill*, in *Works*, 2: 438.

[7] Burke, *Speech on Conciliation*, in *Works*, 2: 145; *Sheriffs of Bristol*, in *Works*, 2: 223, 236; *Address to the British Colonists . . .* , in *Works*, 6: 192.

this shift in Burke's theory of civil society can be seen as early as 1772 in his interpretation of the Act of Union. If any public measure might be represented as a contractual bargain, the act which united England and Scotland certainly qualifies. Yet Burke refused to admit that the terms of union were either "eternally binding" or "absolutely irreversible" in any point. He acknowledged that the act was a solemn and important measure. It was not to be changed without weighty reasons. But he denied that it restricted Parliament's authority in any particular. "The power of rectifying the most sacred laws must, by the very nature of things, be vested in the legislature; because every legislature must be supreme and omnipotent with respect to the law, which is its own creature." The only check that Burke acknowledged on the authority of Parliament arose from considerations of prudence.[8] Clearly the state which Burke assumed here was not the same institution that he had assumed in the *Popery Laws*. In the *Popery Laws* the state lacked dormant and irresistible powers; here it possessed them; in the *Popery Laws*, the state could limit its authority by its engagements; here it could not.

The new conception that Burke had adopted was the trust. His earliest reference to the trust is found in the *Observations on a Late Publication* which he published in 1769.[9] Afterwards his use of the figure was frequent and explicit. In *The Present Discontents*, he wrote of King, Lords, and Commons as "trustees for the people." "No power," he added, "is given for the sole sake of the holder. . . ."[10] In his speech on the surrender of St. Eustatius, he argued that "in all government there is a trust reposed. 'Shew me a government, . . . and I will shew a trust' . . . ."[11] The trust figured in his speech on economic reform. Burke argued that the King's property was held in trust for the people. "The king was only a trustee for the public. Property and subjects existed before kings were elected, and endowed with a portion of the former for the protection of the latter."[12] The trust appears in his Indian speeches. In the debate on Fox's East India bill, Burke argued that no government possessed "original, self-derived rights." The rights and powers of government were all "in the strictest sense *a trust*."[13] The trust was assumed in his earliest attacks on the French Revolution. He wrote in the *Reflections*, "All persons possessing any portion of power ought to be strongly and awfully impressed with an idea that they act in trust, and that they are to account for their conduct

[8] Burke, *Speeches*, 1: 95.

[9] Burke, *Observations on a Late Publication*, in *Works*, 1: 398.

[10] Burke, *The Present Discontents*, in *Works*, 1: 492.

[11] Burke, *Speeches*, 2: 257.

[12] Ibid., 2: 121.

[13] Burke, *Speech on Fox's East India Bill*, in *Works*, 2: 439.

in that trust to the one great Master, Author, and Founder of society."[14] In the later anti-Jacobin works the trust yielded to the corporation. But for all practical purposes the trust supplied Burke with his normal working-conception of what the state was.

Whether this trust is a temporal or a heavenly institution makes little difference for our understanding of its significance. It was not in any strict sense a democratic conception of the state. Even if we suppose that its origins were entirely temporal, Burke's trust does not become a democratic institution. It implies no right on the part of the people to govern, even if it was the people who had settled authority in trust to be administered for their own benefit. For the legal ownership of a trust property belongs not to the settlor, nor to the beneficiary, but to the trustee.[15] Burke's subject either as settlor or as beneficiary could not claim a right to administer the trust at will. Short of extraordinary occasions when the trust was betrayed and rebellion justified, Burke's trustee was not answerable to anyone's discretion for his management. Burke's governors had ceased to be procurators and agents acting on behalf of their subjects as principals. This is clear from the *Reflections* where we find Burke writing:

> Kings, in one sense, are undoubtedly the servants of the people, because their power has no other rational end than that of the general advantage; but it is not true that they are, in the ordinary sense, (by our Constitution, at least,) anything like servants,—the essence of whose situation is to obey the commands of some other, and to be removable at pleasure. But the king of Great Britain obeys no other person; all persons are individually, and collectively too, under him, and owe to him a legal obedience.

What was true of the King, in Burke's opinion, was also true of the Lords and Commons.[16] Moreover, what was true of government under the British constitution was true of all governments under any constitution. As long as the state survived, the supreme power was not answerable for its conduct in office. "It is not merely so in this or that government, but in all countries."[17]

This assumption of independence was crucial to Burke's theory of parliamentary representation. The member of Parliament was raised to a trust by his constituents.[18] Yet within the limits of his trust, Burke's member was not commanded by the wishes of his constituents. He could not in conscience be bound by their mandates or instructions. He was not to act as their agent, their ambassador, or their advocate. His

[14] Burke, *Reflections*, in *Works*, 3: 354.

[15] Keeton, *The Law of Trusts*, p. 246.

[16] Burke, *Reflections*, in *Works*, 3: 269.

[17] Burke, *Impeachment Speech in Opening*, in *Works*, 9: 459-60.

[18] Burke, *Speech on Presenting . . . a Plan for the Economical Reformation of the Civil and Other Establishments*, in *Works*, 2: 281 (hereafter cited as *Speech on Economical Reform*).

duty extended to the welfare of the entire nation.[19] He was a "trustee for the *whole*, and not for the parts."[20] In the last resort the member could not sacrifice his judgment nor his responsibility to the will of the people. "We are not to go to school to them," Burke told the Commons, "to learn the principles of law and government. In doing so, we should not dutifully serve, but we should basely and scandalously betray the people, who are not capable of this service by nature, nor in any instance called to it by the Constitution."[21]

As beneficiary of a trust, the subject in Burke's theory could claim no right to administer that trust. But as beneficiary the subject's equitable rights were immense. The people might demand from the sovereign "an entire devotion to their interest."[22] If government was a contrivance of human wisdom to provide for human wants, then men had a right "that these wants should be provided for by this wisdom."[23] "... All political power which is set over men ... ought to be ... exercised ultimately for their benefit."[24] On the assumption that government was a trust, Burke could argue that it was the exclusive right of the trustee to decide what was of advantage or benefit to the subject. But on the same assumption Burke could also argue that the subject had a right to whatever measures might be thought beneficial or advantageous. The subject possessed no legal right to prescribe policies to the sovereign; he had nevertheless an equitable right to those policies which the sovereign had an obligation to adopt. By the assertion of this equitable right Burke's trust could supply arguments that appeared almost Jacobin in character. "The object of the state is (as far as may be) the happiness of the whole ... and the happiness or misery of mankind, estimated by their feelings and sentiments, and not by any theories of their rights, is, and ought to be, the standard for the conduct of legislators towards the people."[25] But this statement does not deprive the legislators of their formal authority; nor does it represent them as the agents of the people. Whatever equitable rights the people enjoyed under the trust, they did not possess the right to govern themselves.

To fulfill the purpose of this trust, Burke's sovereign commanded an almost unlimited discretion. At times it was both his right and his duty to disregard the restrictions of positive law. On Burke's account, the public welfare was the cause and reason of all law. "Law, being only made for the benefit of the community, cannot in any one of its parts

[19] Burke, *Speech to the Electors of Bristol* ... , in *Works*, 2: 96.

[20] Burke, *Reflections*, in *Works*, 3: 481.

[21] Burke, *Speech for a Bill for Shortening the Duration of Parliaments*, in *Works*, 7: 74.

[22] Burke, *Reflections*, in *Works*, 3: 355.

[23] Ibid., 310.

[24] Burke, *Speech on Fox's East India Bill*, in *Works*, 2: 439.

[25] Burke, *Speech ... upon the Occasion of a Petition of the Unitarian Society*, in *Works*, 7: 45 (hereafter cited as *Speech on the Unitarian Petition).*

resist a demand which may comprehend the total of the public interest."[26] If an emergency occurred that threatened the safety and welfare of the people, the sovereign might disregard positive law. "Every consideration, except what had a tendency to promote these great objects, became superseded—*Salus populi suprema lex, prima lex, media lex*."[27] This discretionary jurisdiction extended even to the forms and the laws of the constitution itself. The constitution was not something that was specified in the terms of the sovereign's trust. It was a prudential contrivance which the sovereign might alter and perhaps was obliged to alter as circumstances dictated. In the American controversy, Burke argued that the constitution had undergone changes in the past. "This Constitution has . . . admitted innumerable improvements, either for the correction of the original scheme . . . or for bringing its principles better to suit those changes which have successively happened in the circumstances of the nation or in the manners of the people." The American crisis required Parliament to consider further changes in the form of the constitution. "Public troubles have often called upon this country to look into its Constitution. It has ever been bettered by such a revision."[28] The trustee's discretion over the forms of the constitution even allowed him to make a valid delegation of his trust. In 1775 Burke urged Parliament to transfer its taxing powers to the colonial assemblies. "If parliament be the sovereign power of America," he argued, "parliament may, by its own act, for wise purposes, put the local power of the purse into other hands than its own, without disclaiming its just prerogative in other particulars."[29] This argument clearly violated the legal maxim that a trustee could not delegate an authority that he possessed in trust. Burke was familiar with the maxim and on occasions appealed to it in argument.[30] The American controversy, however, left Burke with little choice. Before 1775 Burke had insisted that Parliament possessed the constitutional right to tax the colonies; after 1775 he attempted to persuade Parliament to surrender this right on prudential grounds. For the sake of consistency, he was forced to suppose that Parliament possessed the authority to delegate its trust.

In the extent of his jurisdiction Burke's sovereign resembled Hobbes's Leviathan. But here the resemblance ends. For Burke's sovereign unlike Hobbes's possessed his authority in trust. He was under an obligation to use whatever rights he possessed on behalf of someone else. Even if Burke's sovereign did not exceed the limits of his

[26] Burke, *Speech on Economical Reform*, in *Works*, 2: 329.

[27] Burke, *Speeches*, 3: 513.

[28] Burke, *Address to the British Colonists*, in *Works*, 6: 193-94.

[29] Burke, *Speeches*, 1: 353.

[30] Burke, *Impeachment Speech in Reply*, in *Works*, 11: 274; *Speeches*, 2: 244; *Correspondence*, 9: 41.

jurisdiction, it was still possible to charge him with tyranny or breach of trust. The discretion that Burke allowed to the sovereign did not license him to commit arbitrary and lawless acts. For it was in the end a "moral," "virtuous," and "equitable" discretion. Like the discretion of a trustee in English law, it was an authority which could be abused; and if it were abused, it could be condemned in equity. "It is not, perhaps, so much by the assumption of unlawful powers as by the unwise or unwarrantable use of those which are most legal, that governments oppose their true end and object. . . ."[31] At the very least Burke's sovereign had to use his powers of discretion in the interest of his subjects; this obligation alone rendered him liable to judgment in equity. "All discretion must be referred to the conservation and benefit of those over whom power is exercised, and therefore must be guided by rules of sound political morality."[32]

Like the trustee in English law, Burke's sovereign was required to show prudence in the administration of his office. "You can hardly state to me a case to which legislature is the most confessedly competent, in which, if the rules of benignity and prudence are not observed, the most mischievous and oppressive things may not be done."[33] The policy that served the advantage of the citizen could not be discovered without a prudential regard for all the circumstances. For this reason, Burke could require the sovereign to make utilitarian calculations in the administration of his authority. Men had a right to the advantages that government could confer. These advantages were often "in balances between differences of good,—in compromises sometimes between good and evil, and sometimes between evil and evil."[34] What prudent policy required could not be abstractly stated nor prescribed before the event. It depended upon the circumstances of the moment; and as these circumstances changed, the dictates of prudence changed as well. Yet in all circumstances the obedience of the sovereign to the dictates of prudence was an obligation of his trust. "A statesman, never losing sight of principles, is to be guided by circumstances; and judging contrary to the exigencies of the moment, he may ruin his country forever."[35] Under this obligation, the governor had a duty to behave in different ways at different times. If he were at war, his duty might require him to tax the colonies. At peace, his duty might require him to refrain from taxation. If he failed in this prudential duty in either set of circumstances, then he might be condemned for breach of trust.

Burke tended to write like a utilitarian when he stressed the prudential duties of the state. It is not surprising, perhaps, that

[31] Burke, *Speech on the Unitarian Petition*, in *Works*, 7: 42.

[32] Burke, *Impeachment Speech in Reply*, in *Works*, 11: 229.

[33] Burke, *Speech on the Unitarian Petition*, in *Works*, 7: 42.

[34] Burke, *Reflections*, in *Works*, 3: 313.

[35] Burke, *Speech on the Unitarian Petition*, in *Works*, 7: 41.

nineteenth-century commentators represented him as a rather muddled exponent of utilitarian ethics. Whether his ethical theory was at bottom utilitarian is not a question that will be explored here. But it is important to understand that nothing that Burke writes about the prudential obligation of the trustee can be cited as evidence of his ethical theory in general. We cannot infer from the fact that Burke's sovereign has utilitarian duties towards the subject, that Burke believed utilitarian duties governed man as man. The obligation of the sovereign to serve the happiness of the subject was a special and artificial duty. It arose from his appointment to a particular trust; it did not necessarily extend beyond the limits of that trust. Burke can commit himself to a utilitarian theory of jurisprudence without at the same time supposing a utilitarian theory of ethics. Furthermore, there is no need to think that Burke's emphasis on the discretionary rights of the sovereign cancels the subject's appeal to natural justice. As trustee, the sovereign's discretion extended only to whatever rights had been given to him in trust. Burke could deny to him any right to arbitrary power on the supposition that no man possessed arbitrary power to confer in trust. "We have no arbitrary power to give, because arbitrary power is a thing which neither any man can hold nor any man can give. No man can lawfully govern himself according to his own will; much less can one person be governed by the will of another."[36] On the supposition that the citizen cannot delegate illegal authority, Burke can avoid the Hobbesian conclusion that the consent of the citizen justifies the crimes of the sovereign. If we assume that Burke's sovereign derives his authority from God and not from the consent of the subject, this still does not give him any right to dispense with the rules of natural justice. "If . . . all dominion of man over man is the effect of the Divine disposition, it is bound by the eternal laws of Him that gave it, with which no human authority can dispense,—neither he that exercises it, nor even those who are subject to it. . . ."[37] Burke's trustee stood in the same relationship to natural justice as the ordinary trustee stood in relationship to English law: both possessed discretionary powers; both bore prudential obligations; but neither on the pretext of discretion or of prudence could violate the rules of higher justice.

The trust was not an idea that Burke had adopted before he entered politics. There is no evidence in his writings that explains how he discovered and why he continued to use it for most of his active political life. However, we can guess at his reasons with a fair measure of certainty. In public life, Burke often found himself in contention with adversaries who could claim acknowledged rights. He tried to

[36] Burke, *Impeachment Speech in Opening*, in *Works*, 9: 455.

[37] Ibid., 456; see also Burke, *Speech . . . upon Certain Points Relative to his Parliamentary Conduct*, in *Works*, 2: 418-19.

defeat the right of Parliament to tax the colonies and the right of the East India Company to administer Bengal. He challenged the right of the King to manage his own revenue, to choose his own servants, and to dissolve Parliament at will. Burke could hardly deny that these rights existed; nor could he deny the title of the authorities who exercised them. In some cases the ownership of the right was manifestly provided for by the British constitution as he and his contemporaries understood it. That the King might appoint ministers or dissolve Parliament was not something that the eighteenth century was prepared to debate. In other cases, the rights that Burke wished to challenge were rights that he had once asserted himself. In defending the Declaratory Act, he had defended the right of Parliament to tax the colonies. Before he turned against Hastings, Burke had made a very strong defence of the charter rights that belonged to the East India Company.[38] Burke could hardly reverse himself and argue that rights which he had once defended did not in fact exist. But he could argue, and argue without inconsistency, that these rights were held in trust. On each occasion, Burke could recognize the right and acknowledge its legal ownership, and then proceed to defeat the exercise of that right by asserting the equitable interest of the beneficiary.

Burke's reasons for adopting the conception of the corporation or body politic are more difficult to fathom. Doubtless the change had something to do with the French Revolution. The use of the corporation was confined almost entirely to his anti-Jacobin works.[39] Before the Revolution Burke had often used the trust on the popular side of public controversies. But it is unlikely that he discarded the trust because it committed him to democratic arguments. Clearly the trust was a conception that could be worked on either side of a conflict between the government and the people. When he chose to dispute the sovereign's authority, he could plead the beneficiary's interest; and he could plead the trustee's legal right when it suited him to dispute the pretensions of the people. The argument that he had used in defence of the Declaratory Act was also applicable in his case against the claims of abstract natural right. Burke was aware of this and relied heavily on the trust argument in the *Reflections*. Here the trust appeared more frequently than the corporation.[40] On the assumption of a trust he argued that sovereigns were the servants of the people; but unlike ordinary servants they could not be dismissed at pleasure.[41] He could argue that the rights of men in government were their advantages but

[38] Burke, *Speeches*, 1: 144, 151, 166, 169, 171-72.

[39] Burke, *Reflections*, in *Works* 3: 258, 359, 417-18; *Appeal*, in *Works*, 4: 134, 170-74; *The Policy of Allies*, in *Works*, 4: 411-12, 421; *Regicide Peace*, in *Works*, 5: 326, 330.

[40] Allusions to the trust are to be found in Burke, *Reflections*, in *Works*, 3: 269, 310, 313, 354, 355, 481; allusion to the corporation occurs in ibid., 258, 359, 417-18.

[41] Ibid., 269.

that they had no right to demand measures which were neither reasonable nor beneficial.[42] Men might demand from government an entire devotion to their interest; they could not demand an abject submission to their will.[43] In fact Burke was not oblivious to the anti-democratic uses of the trust.

To understand the limitations of the trust we must remember that Burke had two points to make about the French Revolution. The first was that man in civil society could not choose his governors by virtue of his natural rights. For this purpose the assumption of the trust was presumably adequate. The second point was that the National Assembly had gained power by usurpation and that the legal government of France remained with the authorities in the old regime.[44] Here it is possible that the trust proved to be an embarrassment. The two points, after all, were not identical. Without supposing that any democratic right resided in the people of France, it could have been argued that the National Assembly possessed a perfectly legitimate authority. The establishment of the Assembly had been consented to by the King and each of the three Estates. At the King's request, the nobility, the clergy, and the commoners had merged themselves into a single legislature. To invalidate the origins of the National Assembly Burke may well have required a new conception of the state. He needed a conception that would allow him to assert the authority of an ancient constitution, to assert it even against the discretion of the formal government. The trust, or at least the kind of trust that Burke had assumed in the American crisis, could not serve this purpose. On the assumption that the state was a trust, Burke had allowed the government to alter its constitution and to delegate its authority. Whatever the merits of this speculation may be, Burke first introduced his new definition of the state into the *Reflections* at a point where he argued that King, Lords, and Commons could not dissolve themselves nor abdicate their respective duties in the government of the realm.[45] The argument was stated with explicit reference to what might happen in England; we may assume that it had some reference to what had actually happened in France.

In common law a corporation derives its being from the act of the sovereign. For obvious reasons, Burke's state as a corporation could not

[42] Ibid., 313.

[43] Ibid., 355.

[44] Ibid., 450-52, 561; Burke, *A Letter to a Member of the National Assembly . . .* , in *Works*, 4: 51, 53-54; *Appeal*, in *Works*, 4: 70, 185; *Thoughts on French Affairs . . .* , in *Works*, 4: 316; *Heads for Consideration . . .* , in *Works*, 4: 391-92; *The Policy of the Allies*, in *Works*, 4: 411-12, 431-33; *Regicide Peace*, in *Works*, 5: 326, 330; 6: 70; *A Letter to the Empress of Russia*, in *Works*, 6: 116; *Speeches*, 4: 9-10; *Correspondence*, 6: 219, 258, 317, 353, 359-62, 365-66; 7: 384, 434.

[45] Burke, *Reflections*, in *Works*, 3: 257-58.

be explained as an institution which had created itself. It arose from the act of the original corporators.[46] Whatever part God played in its creation, man was at least its "proximate and efficient cause."[47] In this sense Burke could argue in the *Reflections* that "society is, indeed, a contract."[48] He could go on to call society a partnership. But the institution he actually described in this famous passage was not a partnership nor in any strict sense a contractual association. But it was a corporation. Like a common-law corporation Burke's state was subordinated to the ends and purposes of its institution.[49] The ends that Burke imagined were large: "it is not a partnership in things subservient only to the gross animal existence of a temporary and perishable nature. It is a partnership in all science, a partnership in all art, a partnership in every virtue and in all perfection."[50] Like a common-law corporation, Burke's state possessed a capacity for endless duration. A legal succession was created which embraced past, present, and future members.[51] "It becomes," wrote Burke, "a partnership not only between those who are living, but between those who are living, those who are dead, and those who are to be born."[52] Finally, states like common-law corporations could not dissolve themselves at pleasure.[53] They are not "morally at liberty, at their pleasure, and on their speculations of a contingent improvement, wholly to separate and tear asunder the bands of their subordinate community, and to dissolve it into an unsocial, uncivil, unconnected chaos of elementary principles." In civil society the making and unmaking of corporations was regulated by rules of positive law. Similarly, higher justice regulated the state corporation. "Each contract of each particular state is but a clause in the great primeval contract of eternal society. . . . " Here, Burke supposed that the authority of natural law controlled the formation and dissolution of states. "This law is not subject to the will of those who, by an obligation above them, and infinitely superior, are bound to submit their will to that law." The only excuse which might justify the dissolution of the state was the necessity of the act. "It is the first and supreme necessity only, a necessity that is not chosen, but chooses, a necessity paramount to deliberation, that admits no discussion and demands no evidence, which alone can justify a resort to anarchy." But the right to dissolve the

[46] Burke, *Appeal*, in *Works*, 4: 169-70, 172-73.

[47] Burke, *Regicide Peace,* in *Works,* 5: 234.

[48] Burke, *Reflections,* in *Works,* 3: 359.

[49] James Grant, *A Practical Treatise on the Law of Corporations in General, as Well Aggregate as Sole* (London: Butterworth's, 1850), p. 13; Holdsworth, *A History of English Law*, 9: 49, 60-61.

[50] Burke, *Reflections*, in *Works*, 3: 359.

[51] Grant, *The Law of Corporations*, pp. 2-4, 10-11, 20.

[52] Burke, *Reflections*, in *Works*, 3: 359; *Appeal*, in *Works*, 4: 134.

[53] Grant, *The Law of Corporations*, pp. 19-20, 306-307.

corporation under the license of necessity did not mean that its members possessed the right to dissolve it at their discretion. "... If that which is only submission to necessity should be made the object of choice, the law is broken, Nature is disobeyed, and the rebellious are outlawed, cast forth, and exiled, from this world of reason, and order."[54]

Starting from the premise that the state was a corporation, Burke developed a powerful argument against the legitimacy of the National Assembly. The Assembly could claim no authority under the constitution of the old body politic. It was nothing more than "a voluntary association" of men who had usurped an unlawful power. "They have not the sanction and authority of the character under which they first met. They have assumed another of a very different nature, and have completely altered and inverted all the relations in which they originally stood. They do not hold the authority they exercise under any constitutional law of the state."[55] In the *Appeal* Burke entertained the supposition that the old body politic had been validly dissolved and that the Assembly claimed legitimacy under the authority of a new incorporation. But even on this argument, it was still possible for Burke to charge the Assembly with usurpation. "When men ... break up the original compact or agreement which gives its corporate form and capacity to a state, they are no longer a people,—they have no longer a corporate existence,—they have no longer a legal coactive force to bind within, nor a claim to be recognized abroad. They are a number of vague, loose individuals, and nothing more." A majority of this disbanded people could not in right make a new corporation which comprehended the whole population of France. The right of a majority to coerce a minority, if it existed, was an artificial right; its exercise supposed the existence of a corporation; it could not be invoked to justify the formation of a new corporate body. Where it existed, this right was in Burke's words "one of the most violent fictions of positive law that ever has been or can be made on the principles of artificial incorporation. Out of civil society Nature knows nothing of it." On the supposition that the old corporation had been validly dissolved, the new corporation could claim no authority over those Frenchmen who did not freely assent to its formation.

> If men dissolve their ancient incorporation in order to regenerate their community, in that state of things each man has a right, if he pleases, to remain an individual. Any number of individuals, who can agree upon it, have an undoubted right to form themselves into a state apart and wholly independent. If any one of these is forced into the fellowship of another, this is conquest and

[54] Burke, *Reflections*, in *Works*, 3: 359-60.
[55] Ibid., 450.

not compact. On every principle which supposes society to be in virtue of a free covenant, this compulsive incorporation must be null and void.[56]

It was not Burke's purpose, however, to admit that the ancient incorporation had in fact been dissolved. The granting of this assumption would not have conferred legitimacy on the National Assembly. But it would have destroyed all claims in right for a restoration of the *émigré* interest. To defend the pretensions of the *émigrés* Burke had to assume that the old corporation endured and that its constitutional representatives were the exiled princes and their adherents. This Burke did without the slightest reservation.

The truth is, that France is out of itself,—the moral France is separated from the geographical. The master of the house is expelled, and the robbers are in possession. If we look for the *corporate people* of France, existing as corporate in the eye and intention of public law, (that corporate people, I mean, who are free to deliberate and to decide, and who have a capacity to treat and conclude,) they are in Flanders, and Germany, in Switzerland, Spain, Italy, and England. There are all the princes of the blood, there are all the orders of the state, there are all the parliaments of the kingdom.[57]

Until his death this argument dominated Burke's case against the French Revolution. Reduced to its simplest terms, it meant that constitutional authority resided with the brothers of Louis XVI and not with the *de facto* powers in Paris. The former were the legal representatives of the French corporation; the latter were nothing more than usurpers.[58] In a sense, Burke's argument against the revolutionaries never entirely depended upon their abuse of power. Their cruelties and follies may have in Burke's mind aggravated their original offence. But there remained, nevertheless, the original crime of having seized an authority to which they did not possess a valid title. Burke's case against the new regime in France, like Paine's case against the old regime in England, was essentially legitimist. Like Paine, and perhaps like everybody else in the eighteenth century, Burke cared too much about the credentials of government and too little about the merits of its policy.

Whatever part God played in the formation of Burke's state, it is clear that divine participation did not rule out the need for human volition and consent. Burke regarded states as artificial combinations; "in their proximate efficient cause," he spoke of them as "the arbitrary productions of the human mind."[59] His state like Filmer's could figure

[56] Burke, *Appeal*, in *Works*, 4: 170-72.

[57] Burke, *The Policy of the Allies*, in *Works*, 4: 421.

[58] Burke, *Thoughts on French Affairs*, in *Works*, 4: 316-17; *Heads for Consideration*, in *Works*, 4: 391-92; *The Policy of the Allies*, in *Works*, 4: 411-12, 416, 431, 433; *Regicide Peace*, in *Works*, 5: 326-28; 330; 6: 15-17; *A Letter to the Empress of Russia*, in *Works*, 6: 116, *Correspondence*, 7: 391-92, 435.

[59] Burke, *Regicide Peace*, in *Works*, 5: 234.

as a supernatural authority, but the similarity between their conceptions is superficial. Filmer's state derived its authority as a direct and special delegation from God. Burke's state was a secular institution to the extent that it was made in history through the voluntary act of its founders. Burke called this voluntary act sometimes a contract,[60] sometimes an agreement,[61] sometimes a compact,[62] and sometimes a trust.[63] Although Burke might write of God as the author and founder of civil society, God was not in any mysterious sense a party to its institution. In the main, God assumes no more important a part in the formation of Burke's state than he does in Locke's. In both theories God figures as the transcendent deity of eighteenth-century conception. For Burke (as for Locke), God who created his nature had disposed man to assume civil obligations. "... He who gave our nature to be perfected by our virtue willed also the necessary means of its perfection: He willed, therefore, the state. ..."[64] Similarly in both theories God is the author of natural law. The sanctity of the civil compact for Locke and for Burke presupposes the authority of this law. "This great law," Burke argued, "does not arise from our conventions and compacts; on the contrary, it gives to our conventions and compacts all the force and sanction they can have."[65] Burke's acknowledgment of God's part in the formation of civil society was not superstitious or mysterious in any sense that eighteenth-century opinion was likely to condemn. Burke's state did not come into existence as a result of God's special and miraculous intervention.

[60] Burke, *Observations on a Late Publication*, in *Works*, 1: 368; *Reflections*, in *Works*, 3: 359; *Appeal*, in *Works*, 4: 121.

[61] Burke, *Reflections*, in *Works*, 3: 258; *Appeal*, in *Works*, 4: 169.

[62] Burke, *Reflections*, in *Works*, 3: 250, 258; *Appeal*, in *Works*, 4: 162, 173; *The Conduct of the Minority*, in *Works*, 5: 45.

[63] Burke, *Reflections*, in *Works*, 3: 310; *Speeches*, 2: 257.

[64] Burke, *Reflections*, in *Works*, 3: 361. John Locke wrote in section 13 of *The Second Treatise*, "... God hath certainly appointed government to restrain the partiality and violence of men." Similarly he wrote in section 77, "God having made man such a creature, that in his own judgment it was not good for him to be alone, put him under strong obligations of necessity, convenience, and inclination to drive him into society ..." (Locke, *The Second Treatise of Civil Government and a Letter Concerning Toleration*, pp. 8, 39). In no trivial sense Locke's God also willed the state.

[65] Burke, *Impeachment Speech in Opening*, in *Works*, 9: 455-56. Locke was no less emphatic than Burke in asserting that the sanctity of promises supposed the authority of divine law. Princes, he argued in section 195 of *The Second Treatise*, "owe subjection to the laws of God and nature. No body, no power, can exempt them from the obligations of that eternal law. Those are so great and so strong in the case of promises that omnipotency itself can be tied by them. Grants, promises, and oaths are bonds that hold the Almighty." He refused toleration to atheists on the grounds that they could not bind themselves by their promises: "Promises, covenants, and oaths, which are the bonds of human society, can have no hold upon an atheist. The taking away of God, though but even in thought, dissolves all ... " (John Locke, *The Second Treatise of Civil Government and a Letter Concerning Toleration*, pp. 96, 156).

Burke's supposition of human consent worked only for the first formation of the state. When he tried to account for the obligations of those citizens who were neither founding-fathers nor express contractors, then the coherence of his explanation collapsed. In *The Conduct of the Minority* it was argued that people submitted to old governments "not because they have chosen them, but because they are born to them."[66] The same argument was stated at greater length in the *Appeal*:

> Though civil society might be at first a voluntary act, (which in many cases it undoubtedly was,) its continuance is under a permanent standing covenant, coexisting with the society; and it attaches upon every individual of that society, without any formal act of his own. This is warranted by the general practice, arising out of the general sense of mankind. Men without their choice derive benefits from that association; without their choice they are subjected to duties in consequence of these benefits; and without their choice they enter into a virtual obligation as binding as any that is actual.[67]

Here, Burke made an effort to keep up the authority of the original contract: the original covenant was said to endure and to attach to subsequent members of the state. The rights and duties of the son were presumably the same as the rights and duties of the father. Yet the assumption which had explained the father's obligation does not explain the son's. The father's attachment to the covenant was voluntary; the son's was not. The son acquired the benefits and duties of civil society without choice; for him the authority of the original contract commenced at birth. In short, the first generation of Burke's citizens entered into civil society by virtue of their free consent; the second generation was conscripted into membership by the forces of nature and the will of God.

Whatever it may have been in its origins, Burke's state at this point ceases to be credible as the institution of human contract and consent. The inconsistency, however, cannot be read to prove that Burke rejected Locke or the characteristic assumptions of contract theory. For the inconsistency was not peculiar to Burke. It is evident in other contract theories; and is perhaps something that no contract theory can really avoid. Locke, for example, started with the supposition that civil obedience arose from consent. Yet without explanation, he assigned to the state a comprehensive territorial jurisdiction. The obligation to obey the laws of Locke's government reached "as far as the very being of any one within the territories of that government."[68] The supposition of consent may give to governments a jurisdiction over men; it

[66] Burke, *The Conduct of the Minority*, in *Works*, 5: 46.

[67] Burke, *Appeal*, in *Works*, 4: 165.

[68] Locke, *The Second Treatise of Civil Government and a Letter Concerning Toleration*, p. 60.

does not give them a jurisdiction over territory. In logic, there is no way to make the non-consenting resident into a subject by virtue of his location. Contract assumptions may explain the origins of the state; but they cannot explain the historical realities of obedience and civil authority. The contractualist must admit that in practice a degree of artificial obligation extends to people who cannot be presumed to have consented to it. In common jurisprudence infants have no capacity for contract; yet in practice infants are subject to the authority of positive law. Vattel on this point ran into exactly the same difficulties as Burke. "Children," Vattel wrote, "have a natural attachment to the society in which they are born: being obliged to acknowledge the protection it has granted to their fathers, they are obliged to it, in a great measure, for their birth and education. They ought then to love it, . . . express a just gratitude to it, and as much as possible return benefit for benefit."[69] Vattel's children, like Burke's, were born to unchosen benefits and in consequence inherited unchosen duties.

Neither Vattel nor Locke believed that the obligations of birth and location were indelible. Both assumed that the child on reaching the age of discretion was free to choose his citizenship.[70] Although this assumption does not explain the obligations of the child, it does salvage the contract explanation for the obligations of the adult. It is not unlikely that Burke made a similar assumption. He had been born an Irishman and became an Englishman by choice. Throughout his life he acknowledged that he owed duties to both England and Ireland. But the artificial and chosen duty to England took priority over his natural duty to Ireland. In 1780 he told his Bristol constituents, "I certainly have very warm good wishes for the place of my birth. But the sphere of my duties is my true country."[71] Five years later he made the same point in the Commons.

> It was true he was an Irishman; and he conceived much was due by everyman to the place of his nativity, but that this duty ought not to absorb every other. When another country was generous enough to receive a man into her bosom, and raise him from nothing, . . . to stations of honour and trust, . . . such a country had claims upon him not inferior to those of that which had given him birth.[72]

[69] Emerich von Vattel, *The Law of Nations: or Principles of the Law of Nature Applied to the Conduct and Affairs of Nations and Sovereigns* (Philadelphia: P. H. Nicklin and T. Johnson, 1829), p. 162.

[70] Ibid.; John Locke, *The Second Treatise of Civil Government and a Letter Concerning Toleration*, p. 59.

[71] Burke, *Speech upon Certain Points Relative to his Parliamentary Conduct*, in *Works*, 2: 377.

[72] Burke, *Speeches*, 3: 193.

In 1792 he again admitted the double obligation. But if the two countries should ever come into conflict, it was with England, "which was the country of his adoption, that he would take part."[73] In Burke's own case the allegiance of choice finally superseded the allegiance of birth and inheritance.

If we consider Burke's theory of the state in its entirety, its basic incoherence cannot be denied. It is impossible to conceive of the citizen as being the principal of an agent, the beneficiary of a trust, and a corporator of a body politic. The legal relationships which these figures imply are radically different. The citizen cannot be all three things at once with respect to the same civil relationships. In a sense, Burke did not develop a consistent theory of the state, but adopted a succession of legal identities which he introduced as the necessities of debate required. But if we admit this, we should also recognize that there were limits to Burke's powers of invention. However much he shifted and changed in his definition of the state, he never went beyond the truisms of eighteenth-century political speculation. Nor did he adopt any conception that places him in fundamental opposition to Locke. Whether Burke's state stands as agent, trust, or corporation, it is a legal institution with rights and duties prescribed by law. It is an institution that man has made under the authority of higher justice. Like Locke (and for that matter like Hobbes and Paine as well) Burke assumed that man outside the state had the capacity to create binding legal relationships. If we grant the premise that man in nature may make a bargain, Burke's supposition that man in nature may make an agency, a trust, or a corporation is not outrageous. Doubtless the supposition of an agency, a trust, or a corporation is more elaborate than the supposition of a simple contract. But once it is admitted that men without the state may create associations that bind them in conscience and may be enforced against their will, it is difficult to prescribe a limit to the variety of associations that they may make. Far from rejecting the distinctive principles of eighteenth-century political theory, Burke had retained them and used them to serve his controversial purposes.

[73] Ibid., 4: 79.

Five

History

The political theory of the eighteenth century often ignored the diversity of men and the variety of circumstances. Political obligation was explained in terms of universal natural law and uniform human nature. It was not until the nineteenth century that man's nature and his rights were commonly thought to be things which history could create and modify. Burke sometimes figures as an eighteenth-century pioneer of this nineteenth-century truth. He sensed that societies differed in their customs and prejudices. He often argued that these differences governed the political rights that were appropriate to each people. "Social and civil freedom . . . are variously mixed and modified, enjoyed in very different degrees, and shaped into an infinite diversity of forms, according to the temper and circumstances of every community."[1] "A wise Prince," he wrote in a private letter, ". . . will study the genius of his people; he will indulge them in their humours, he will preserve them in their privileges; he will act upon the *circumstances of his states as he finds them*. . . ."[2] Such acknowledgment of the importance of man's historical peculiarities perhaps testifies to Burke's shrewdness and common sense. But it leaves us with the problem of explaining how he could appear to write like an historical relativist of the nineteenth century and not violate his eighteenth-century commitment to natural justice and contract theory.

[1] Burke, *Sheriffs of Bristol*, in *Works*, 2: 229.

[2] Burke, *Correspondence*, 6: 267-68.

When Burke wrote *The Sublime and Beautiful*, he assumed that human nature was in certain respects constant and unchanging. The study of taste, he thought, supposed that men were identical in their basic psychology. Otherwise, ". . . it must be judged an useless, if not an absurd undertaking, to lay down rules for caprice, and to set up for a legislator of whims and fancies." Men might exhibit differences in their reasonings and pleasures, but such differences were rather "apparent than real." " . . . If there were not some principles of judgment as well as of sentiment common to all mankind, no hold could possibly be taken either on their reason or their passions, sufficient to maintain the ordinary correspondence of life."[3] This identity embraced man's perceptions and passions. Because men were the same in their anatomy, he supposed that they were the same in their perception of the external world. "We are satisfied that what appears to be light to one eye, appears light to another; that what seems sweet to one palate, is sweet to another. . . ." To deny that men were identical in their perception of reality would make "every sort of reasoning on every subject vain and frivolous." Men were also identical in their primary feelings of pleasure and pain: ". . . the pleasures and the pains which every object excites in one man, it must raise in all mankind, whilst it operates naturally, simply, and by its proper powers only. . . ." The same cause acting in the same manner on subjects of the same kind could not conceivably produce different effects.[4] Imagination served to represent the senses. It was the region "of our fears and our hopes, and of all our passions that are connected with them." Whatever affected the imagination of one man exerted "the same power pretty equally over all men." The images of things, explained Burke, give to the imagination pleasure or pain on the same principle "on which the sense is pleased or displeased with the realities." ". . . Consequently there must be just as close an agreement in the imaginations as in the senses of men."[5] Finally he assumed the identity of men in their passions. Love, grief, fear, anger, joy were felt by every man. These passions did not affect the mind "in an arbitrary or casual manner," but worked upon "certain, natural, and uniform principles."[6]

Burke never seriously repudiated this assumption of human identity. In the impeachment of Hastings he might sometimes argue as if the English and the Indians were fundamentally different. The two races, he supposed, were divorced by "inveterate habits as strong as nature itself." They were separated by "what may be considered as a

[3] Burke, *The Sublime and Beautiful*, in *Works*, 1: 79-80.

[4] Ibid., 82-83.

[5] Ibid., 87.

[6] Ibid., 94.

diversity even in the very constitution of their minds."[7] But however sensitive he was to the peculiarities of Indian culture, Burke's basic argument in the impeachment was that Indians and Englishmen exhibited a common human nature. Whatever the diversities may have been he called upon the Englishman to understand the Indian as a natural man. He called upon the Lords to feel a sympathetic revengefulness on behalf of the Indian.[8] He denied that it could be common custom for Indians to sell their children into servitude. If the Indians ever sold their children, it was proof of Hastings' oppressiveness. "No man ever sold his children but under the pressure of some cruel exaction. Nature calls out against it."[9] The very charge that he made against Hastings in the peroration of the opening speech supposed that Hastings had violated the common nature of man. "I impeach him in the name of human nature itself, which he has cruelly outraged, injured, and oppressed, in both sexes, in every age, rank, situation, and condition of life."[10] From the beginning to the end of his career, Burke asserted the reality of an abstract and uniform human nature.

The differences that distinguished historical men did not arise from a fundamental variety in the constitution of their minds. They arose from habits, opinions, and prejudices that men acquired and formed what Burke was to call man's second nature. "Man, in his moral nature, becomes, in his progress through life, a creature of prejudice, a creature of opinions, a creature of habits, and of sentiments growing out of them. These form our second nature, as inhabitants of the country and members of the society in which Providence has placed us."[11] The diversity in man's second nature was created by the varied circumstances of life. Differences of birth, education, occupation, residence, and laws combined to make men "as it were, so many different species of animals."[12] In *The Sublime and Beautiful* Burke had explained second nature in the acquisition of customary and peculiar appetites. In their natural state, men agreed in their sense of pain and pleasure: sweetness was pleasant and sourness unpleasant. Yet in practice, he argued, men often deviate from the natural taste: the Turk liked opium; the Dutchman liked tobacco; and the Englishman liked spirits. The flavour of these luxuries would have been "absolutely neglected if their properties had originally gone no further than the taste." Burke supposed that opium, tobacco, and spirits were first taken for their

[7] Burke, *Report from the Committee Appointed to Inspect the Lords' Journals*, in *Works*, 11: 61-62.

[8] Burke, *Impeachment Speech on the Sixth Article*, in *Works*, 10: 311; *Impeachment Speech in Reply*, in *Works*, 11: 179-81.

[9] Burke, *Impeachment Speech in Reply*, in *Works*, 11: 422.

[10] Burke, *Impeachment Speech in Opening,* in *Works,* 10: 145.

[11] Burke, *Impeachment Speech in Reply,* in *Works,* 12: 164.

[12] Burke, *Reflections*, in *Works*, 3: 476-77.

utility as drugs. Their value as drugs influenced the natural appetite by force of association. "The effect of the drug has made us use it frequently; and frequent use, combined with the agreeable effect, has made the taste itself at last agreeable."[13] The acquired appetite had its origin in utility. The continued indulgence of that taste was accounted for on the supposition that man found it painful to interrupt any of his acquired habits. "It is the nature of things which hold us by custom, to affect us very little whilst we are in possession of them, but strongly when they are absent." The snuff-taker uses snuff without consciousness of pleasure; yet, deprived of his box, he feels distress.

> Very justly is use called a second nature; and our natural and common state is one of absolute indifference, equally prepared for pain or pleasure. But when we are thrown out of this state, or deprived of anything requisite to maintain us in it . . . we are always hurt. It is so with the second nature, custom, in all things which relate to it.[14]

To go from an explanation of acquired tastes to an explanation of acquired opinions and prejudices is to take a rather long step in argument. Burke does not give us a systematic account of how this step was taken. But in essential respects Burke's habitual prejudice resembles the habitual appetite. Both contribute to the formation of man's second nature. They both supply him with a new source of feeling and a capacity for pain that he lacked in his original and natural state. "We know what the empire of opinion is in human nature. . . ." Burke argued in the impeachment, "It is . . . the strongest principle in the composition of the frame of the human mind; and more of the happiness and unhappiness of mankind resides in that inward principle than in all external circumstances put together."[15] The snuff-taker deprived of his box felt distress from the interruption of his habit; similarly a person offended in his habitual prejudices could feel an injury more acute than the injuries to his physical nature. The misery felt by Indians that arose from the violation of their caste exceeded the pain of physical torture. "The dominion of manners and the law of opinion contribute more to their happiness and misery than anything in mere sensitive nature can do."[16]

An initial merit in utility had been supposed by Burke to explain the origin of the habitual appetite. In the *Reflections*, he grounded his defence of prejudice on an assumption of its "latent wisdom." It was the business of the philosopher not to discredit prejudices but "to discover

[13] Burke, *The Sublime and Beautiful*, in *Works*, 1: 85-86.

[14] Ibid., 179-80.

[15] Burke, *Impeachment Speech in Opening*, in *Works*, 9: 379; *Impeachment Speech in Reply*, in *Works*, 12: 164.

[16] Burke, *Impeachment Speech in Opening*, in *Works*, 10: 89.

the latent wisdom which prevails in them." "If they find what they seek, (and they seldom fail,)" Burke argued, "they think it more wise to continue the prejudice, with the reason involved, than to cast away the coat of prejudice, and to leave nothing but the naked reason. . . ."[17] In the prejudices of chivalry and religion, Burke stated the latent wisdom that accounted for the affection in their favour. Chivalry, he argued, softened the relationships between the sovereign and the subject. "It was this, which, without confounding ranks, had produced a noble equality, and handed it down through all the gradations of social life. . . ."[18] Religion was a prejudice that involved "profound and extensive wisdom." Among its many merits, it persuaded civil man that he acted in trust and was accountable to God for the use of his public authority.[19] Latent wisdom could be presumed in favour of opinions and prejudices even in instances where Burke did not care to demonstrate it. On the eve of the French Revolution, Europe was prosperous. "How much of the prosperous state was owing to the spirit of our old manners and opinions is not easy to say," he admitted, "but as such causes cannot be indifferent in their operation, we must presume, that, on the whole, their operation was beneficial."[20] The mere survival and persistence of habitual peculiarities suggested that they might possess a merit in reason. The customs and opinions of the Indians had survived centuries of conquest and invasion. "This alone," Burke concluded, "furnishes full proof that there must be some powerful influence resulting from them beyond all our little fashionable theories upon such subjects."[21]

Man's affection for an habitual taste did not depend upon his knowledge or recollection of its original utility. Similarly, his affection for his customary prejudices and opinions sprang from the force of habit and not necessarily from the reasons that might justify the habit. The impulse of prejudice could act upon a man who was unconscious of its latent wisdom. "Prejudice is of ready application in the emergency; it previously engages the mind in a steady course of wisdom and virtue. . . . Prejudice renders a man's virtue his habit, and not a series of unconnected acts. Through just prejudice, his duty becomes a part of his nature."[22] Quite apart from any presumed merit or justification, prejudice could exercise an influence upon man's mind and his feelings. For this reason, Burke could go on to argue that prejudice and custom should be respected even in instances where he

[17] Burke, *Reflections*, in *Works*, 3: 346.
[18] Ibid., 332.
[19] Ibid., 352-56.
[20] Ibid., 335.
[21] Burke, *Impeachment Speech in Opening*, in *Works*, 9: 383.
[22] Burke, *Reflections*, in *Works*, 3: 347.

did not choose to suppose that they were justified by latent wisdom. In the American controversy, he contended that government should conform to the general prejudices of the people, "... even where the foundation of such prejudices may be false or disputable."[23] Respect for the Indian prejudice of caste did not in the last resort depend upon the merit of the prejudice in reason. "We are not here to commend or blame the institutions and prejudices of a whole race of people, radicated in them by a long succession of ages, on which no reason or argument, on which no vicissitudes of things ... have been able to make the smallest impression."[24] A prejudice might reflect the latent wisdom which justified it; but even if it did not, it was still an area of feeling in which the natural man felt pleasure and pain. To this extent it possessed a claim upon the statesman's consideration.

The opinions and prejudices that were held throughout an entire society formed for Burke the basis of its distinctive character. Burke gave this character many names. He called it the "sense" of the people, their "genius," or their "spirit."[25] Sometimes it was their "general opinion," their "public inclination," their "general feelings," or their "national character."[26] In its conception, Burke's national character was completely individualistic. It was the effect rather than the cause of the peculiarities of particular citizens. Having supposed that man was imitative and admiring by nature, there was no need for Burke to invent a collective consciousness or national soul.[27] Nor was there any need for him to imagine that men's minds undergo organic modification in the course of history. Novel customs and opinions might be transmitted by the influence of one natural man acting upon the deference of another.

> The mass of Mankind are made to be led by others.... Subordination ... is necessary for the human mind. Men, long after they have left their state of Nature, still require guides through Life. Habits, therefore, are adopted for the Multitude. Authority is enough for most of those who if they cannot think themselves, can be supported by habits & Examples.[28]

National character for Burke might be modified just as the distinctive character of any individual might be modified. Neither was the consequence of biological inheritance. Whether he represented the character of a society as fixed or fluid depended a great deal upon the

[23] Burke, *Address to the King*, in *Works*, 6: 165.

[24] Burke, *Impeachment Speech in Opening*, in *Works*, 10: 89.

[25] Burke, *Speeches*, 3: 10; *Correspondence*, 6: 267; *Speech on Conciliation*, in *Works*, 2: 127.

[26] Burke, *Sheriffs of Bristol*, in *Works*, 2: 224-25; *Address to the King*, in *Works*, 6: 165; *Impeachment Speech on the Sixth Article*, in *Works*, 10: 450.

[27] Burke, *The Sublime and Beautiful*, in *Works*, 1: 122-23.

[28] Burke, *Extracts from Mr. Burke's Table-Talk Written Down by Mrs. Crewe* (London: Philobiblion Society, 1862), p. 56.

point that he was arguing. In India the social habits of the natives were "inveterate" and as "strong as nature itself."[29] In America the temper and character of the colonists were "unalterable by any human art."[30] But in England it often suited Burke to depict national character as something that could be transformed by any bad example that he had chosen to condemn. He warned that the acquittal of Hastings would transform English virtues into Indian vices. The English, he said, had the character of being "an open-hearted, candid, liberal, plain, sincere people." But if the Lords connived at Hastings' crimes, they would teach the English public "a concealing, narrow, suspicious, guarded conduct." ". . . If you teach them qualities directly the contrary to those by which they have hitherto been distinguished," he told the Lords, "—if you make them a nation of concealers, a nation of dissemblers, a nation of liars, a nation of forgers . . . if you, in one word, turn them into a people of *banians*, the character of England . . . will be gone and lost."[31] Later, in his attack on the French Revolution, he warned that the character of England was threatened by the example of France. Little was to be feared from the military power of the French; but a great deal was to be feared "from the example of a people whose character knows no medium." The danger was that the people of England might be led "through an admiration of successful fraud and violence" into an imitation of French excesses.[32]

Burke often insisted that the state should consult and even take steps to preserve the character of the people. However, he rarely permitted it to play a positive role in the creation of that character. What he called "the circumstances of civil life" might allow man to acquire habits, manners, and prejudices that he did not possess in nature.[33] But this development occurred in consequence of man's natural aptitudes and not as a consequence of government policy and official initiation. To the acquisition of manners politicians may "give a leaning, but they cannot give a law."[34] The true end of government, as it was stated in the *Sheriffs of Bristol*, was "to follow, not to force, the public inclination,—to give a direction, a form, a technical dress, and a specific sanction, to the general sense of the community."[35] In the *Letter to a Noble Lord* he argued that the prejudice which men felt in favour of old nobility was not a consequence of formal legislation: ". . . *the thing itself* is matter of *inveterate* opinion, and therefore *cannot* be matter of mere

[29] Burke, *Report from the Committee Appointed to Inspect the Lords' Journals*, in *Works*, 11: 61.

[30] Burke, *Speech on Conciliation*, in *Works*, 2: 133.

[31] Burke, *Burke, Speech on the Sixth Article*, in *Works*, 10: 450.

[32] Burke, *The Speech in the Debate on the Army Estimates. . .* , in *Works*, 3: 216-18.

[33] Burke, *Reflections*, in *Works*, 3: 476-77.

[34] Burke, *Thoughts on Scarcity*, in *Works*, 5: 167.

[35] Burke, *Sheriffs of Bristol*, in *Works*, 2: 225.

positive institution."[36] If it was the duty of government to respect and defend the character that nature ordained, the state should not presume to foster a new character which might be preferred on speculative grounds. To force the habits and circumstances of a country, Burke argued, was "always perilous and productive of the greatest calamities."[37]

The attack on the Irish penal laws derived in part from Burke's prohibition against the artificial legislation of manners. In the *Popery Laws* he argued that the effort to turn Catholics into Protestants was doomed to failure. The Catholics of Ireland were behaving naturally in giving an "implicit admiration and adherence" to the opinions of their forefathers. Those opinions might be faulty and erroneous; the inculcation of Protestant doctrines might be regarded as a social improvement. Nevertheless, "veneration of antiquity is congenial to the human mind." Irish Catholicism was "an opinion in possession." In its efforts to destroy that opinion, the state had aroused against itself "all the powerful prejudices of human nature." The legislation of the penal laws had served to make matters worse. The state had found the people of Ireland as "heretics and idolaters"; its policy of coercive conversion had turned them into "slaves and beggars." ". . . They remain in all the misfortune of their old errors, and all the superadded misery of their recent punishment."[38] In his later Irish works Burke shifted his ground. Writing in the 1790s he admitted the possibility that the state might persecute the Irish "out of their prejudices." But this possibility did not justify the policy of official conversion. The state might conceivably destroy one set of prejudices in the minds of its subjects; but the state could not hope to replace it with another set. "If anything is, one more than another, out of the power of man, it is to *create* a prejudice."[39] Disturbed in their affection for Catholicism, the Irish would turn to Jacobinism and atheism and not to any of the Protestant churches. "Depend upon it," Burke wrote to Langrishe, "it is as true as Nature is true, that, if you force them out of the religion of habit, education, or opinion, it is not to yours they will ever go. Shaken in their minds, they will go to that where the dogmas are fewest. . . ."[40]

Burke's argument against Jacobin policy in France resembled his argument against Protestant policy in Ireland. The Jacobins, like the Protestants, were committed to an effort to destroy the rooted prejudices and manners of the people.[41] The new prejudices favoured by

[36] Burke, *A Letter to a Noble Lord . . .*, in *Works*, 5: 225.

[37] Burke, *Appeal*, in *Works*, 4: 109; *Letter to Richard Burke . . .*, in *Works*, 6: 402.

[38] Burke, *Popery Laws*, in *Works*, 6: 337-41.

[39] Burke, *A Letter to William Smith on the Subject of Catholic Emancipation*, in *Works*, 6: 368.

[40] Burke, *Letter to Langrishe*, in *Works*, 4: 299.

[41] Burke, *Letter to William Smith*, in *Works*, 6: 367.

the Protestants were presumably blameless and perhaps even preferable to Catholic doctrine. The error for Burke lay not in Protestantism itself, but in the effort to spread a good doctrine by artificial means.[42] In France, however, Jacobin manners were bad in themselves. The Jacobins had "settled a system of manners, the most licentious, prostitute, and abandoned that ever has been known."[43] Their system encouraged a hardening of the heart and the relaxation of morals. It is "at war with all orderly and moral society, and is in its neighborhood unsafe."[44] On Burke's account, the French aspired to effect a "regeneration of the moral constitution of man." The new man which they contrived to make was a creature of artificial invention. "Statesmen like your present rulers," he wrote in the *Letter to a Member of the National Assembly*, "exist by everything which is spurious, fictitious, and false,—by everything which takes the man from his house, and sets him on a stage,—which makes him up an artificial creature, with painted, theatric sentiments, fit to be seen by the glare of candle-light, and formed to be contemplated at a due distance."[45] The theme of artificiality and contrivance in the formation of manners was again developed by Burke in the *Regicide Peace*: "Nothing in the Revolution, no, not to a phrase or a gesture, not to the fashion of a hat or a shoe, was left to accident. All has been the result of design; all has been matter of institution. No mechanical means could be devised in favor of this incredible system of wickedness and vice, that has not been employed."[46] In the name of civic duty, the people were disciplined into an artificial ferocity of manners and conduct. "To this ferocity there is joined not one of the rude, unfashioned virtues which accompany the vices, where the whole are left to grow up together in the rankness of uncultivated Nature. But nothing is left to Nature in their systems."[47] In France as in Ireland, Burke's defence of historic prejudices, manners, and customs amounted to little more than an argument that whatever nature prescribed is best left to nature's jurisdiction. It is a standard eighteenth-century plea that men should follow nature in their artificial contrivances.

Burke often supposed that the character of the people governed the degree of constitutional liberty which they were entitled to in civil government. Civil freedom in general was "a blessing and a benefit." It was a "good to be improved, and not an evil to be lessened." The duty of the statesman obliged him to discover how much civil freedom the

[42] Burke, *Popery Laws*, in *Works*, 6: 339-40.
[43] Burke, *Regicide Peace*, in *Works*, 5: 310.
[44] Ibid., 317.
[45] Burke, *Letter to a Member of the National Assembly*, in *Works*, 4: 28.
[46] Burke, *Regicide Peace*, in *Works*, 5: 311.
[47] Ibid., 315-16.

people could profitably enjoy.[48] "The general character and situation of a people must determine what sort of government is fitted for them. That point nothing else can or ought to determine."[49] ". . . The circumstances and habits of every country . . . are to decide upon the form of its government."[50] It was the duty of the British government to conform "to the character and circumstances of the several people" who made up the empire. Institutions which were appropriate to the administration of Bengal were not appropriate for the administration of New England.[51] The right of the people to a government fitted to their character and the duty of the sovereign to provide that form of government was not something that could be alienated by compact. Even if the American colonists had formally surrendered all their claims to civil liberty, such a surrender on Burke's account did not justify the statesman in withholding the civil liberties that were appropriate to their general character. "I should hold myself obliged to conform to the temper I found universally prevalent in my own day, and to govern two million of men, impatient of servitude, on the principles of freedom."[52]

When Burke stated his case against American taxation, he did not suppose that the colonists had possessed a formal or constitutional right that Parliament had violated. Such a supposition would have made nonsense of the Declaratory Act. Burke appealed not to any civil right that the Americans actually possessed by virtue of the constitution but to a civil right which they ought to be granted by virtue of their general character. That character, as it was described in the *Speech on Conciliation*, exhibited a fierce spirit of liberty. All the circumstances of history had combined to make the love of liberty stronger among the colonists than among any other people in the world. The colonists were descended from Englishmen; and like Englishmen, they associated civil freedom with the right to grant taxes to the sovereign. In New England, the colonists adhered to Congregationalism. Dissenters of all kinds disliked government and favoured civil freedom. This disposition found its strongest expression among the Congregationalists. Congregationalism was "a refinement on the principle of resistance: it is the dissidence of dissent, and the protestantism of the Protestant religion." In the south, the colonists owned slaves. The presence of slavery made men jealous of their liberty. "In such a people, the haughtiness of domination combines with the spirit of freedom, fortifies it, and renders it invincible."[53] Out of these and other historical circumstances

[48] Burke, *Sheriffs of Bristol*, in *Works*, 2: 229.
[49] Burke, *Speech on Conciliation*, in *Works*, 2: 141.
[50] Burke, *Appeal*, in *Works*, 4: 109.
[51] Burke, *Sheriffs of Bristol*, in *Works*, 2: 227.
[52] Burke, *Speech on Conciliation*, in *Works*, 2: 141.
[53] Ibid., 120-24.

the American character was formed; and once formed, it could not be modified by the power of the state. The offending taxes had to be abandoned. "No way is open . . . but . . . to comply with the American spirit as necessary, or, if you please, to submit to it as a necessary evil."[54]

In its essentials this argument was repeated by Burke in his attack on the French Revolution. If the Americans by virtue of their character deserved free institutions, the French by virtue of theirs qualified for despotism. On first learning of the revolution, Burke expressed alarm that the "old Parisian ferocity" had again erupted. It signified nothing if that eruption had been accidental. "But if it should be character rather than accident, then that people are not fit for Liberty, and must have a Strong hand like that of their former masters to coerce them." In order to qualify for civil freedom men had to exhibit a degree of "natural moderation."[55] The later course of the revolution quickly confirmed Burke's doubts: the excesses sprang not from accident but from the character and temper of the people. "Why speculate on the measure and standard of liberty?" he asked, "I doubt much, very much indeed, whether France is at all ripe for liberty on any standard." Man deserved civil liberty to the extent that he could put "moral chains" upon his appetite. The less he could control himself, the more he had to be controlled by the state. "It is ordained in the eternal constitution of things, that men of intemperate minds cannot be free. Their passions forge their fetters."[56] Far from manifesting a spirit of liberty, the French had revealed the disposition of tyrants. They thirsted "for blood and confiscation in the bosom of Peace." Such men were made to be slaves. "It is good for themselves and for everyone else that they should be so."[57]

It is doubtful, however, that Burke advised a blind obedience to whatever national character the accidents of history created. The relativist implications of his American and French arguments find a contradiction in his case for the Catholic franchise. Here he did not base his claims upon any appeal to the Irish national character. He might condemn policies that were calculated to amend that character, but he never argued that the Irish like the Americans qualified for civil freedom by virtue of their temperament and disposition. To understand this omission, we must remember that the character of the Irish Catholics was hardly appropriate to the case that Burke argued on their behalf. He could not tell a generation of Whigs that the Irish exhibited a fierce spirit of liberty. At the time of the Glorious Revolution, the Irish Catholics had fought against "liberty" and for "despotism." Indeed, there was little that could have been said on behalf of the Irish

[54] Ibid., 139.

[55] Burke, *Correspondence*, 6: 10.

[56] Burke, *Letter to a Member of the National Assembly*, in *Works*, 4: 51-52.

[57] Burke, *Correspondence*, 6: 108.

Catholics that did not find its contradiction in the *Speech on Conciliation*. There Burke had assumed that Protestantism disposed men to favour civil freedom and he strongly implied that Catholicism disposed them to suffer despotic government.[58] The Irish Catholics could not qualify as the descendants of Englishmen. Nor could they qualify as haughty slaveowners. Burke's representative Irishmen were in his words "drawers of water and cutters of turf."[59] Ireland, itself, was "an enslaved, beggard, insulted, degraded Catholick Country."[60] The fierce spirit of liberty that he had discovered in America was very much the peculiarity of an English, Protestant, and aristocratic population. It was not to be found in a population of Irish, Catholic, peasants. "There may be a party spirit," he wrote of Ireland, "but public spirit there can be none. As to a spirit of liberty, still less can it exist, or anything like it."[61] The absence of an appropriate national character was explained by Burke on the grounds that the Catholic population had been the victims of persecution and oppression. "Are we to be astonished," he asked Langrishe, "when, by the efforts of so much violence in conquest, and so much policy in regulation, continued without intermission for near an hundred years, we had reduced them to a mob, that, whenever they came to act at all, many of them would act exactly like a mob, without temper, measure, or foresight?"[62] But the fact remains that on the grounds of their historical character the Irish Catholics were no more fitted for the enjoyment of civil freedom than were the French. In America, Burke had stressed the dictates of the historical character as if it were the decisive consideration; in France, he urged it as an important consideration; in Ireland, it was a consideration which he absolutely ignored. Here the object of public policy was to correct the blunders that history had made.

Burke's preoccupation with the historical peculiarities of people owes a great deal to Montesquieu and little to Locke. We should not, however, interpret Burke's emphasis on historical character as a contradiction of his commitments either to natural justice or to the contract theory of the state. Important as historical peculiarities were, Burke never assigned to them a legislative authority. He might argue that prejudices, manners, and opinions could possess a redeeming merit; he often argued that they should not be wantonly offended by government; but in the end he did not argue that history specified justice. The presumption that history created or revealed right was expressly denied in a private letter. "My principles enable me to form my judge-

[58] Burke, *Speech on Conciliation*, in *Works*, 2: 122.

[59] Burke, *Letter to Langrishe*, in *Works*, 4: 246-47.

[60] Burke, *Correspondence*, 7: 118.

[61] Burke, *Letter to Richard Burke*, in *Works*, 6: 389.

[62] Burke, *Letter to Langrishe*, in *Works*, 4: 247; *Letter to Richard Burke*, in *Works*, 6: 389.

ment upon Men and Actions in History, just as they do in current life; and are not formed out of events and Characters, either present or past. History is a preceptor of Prudence not of principles. The principles of true politicks are those of morality enlarged, and I neither now do or ever will admit of any other."[63] He could imagine that there were such things as bad customs and that it was the duty of the good statesman to disregard them. In the impeachment of Hastings, Burke denied that the custom of the East could excuse bribery. "I remember Lord Coke, talking of the Brehon law in Ireland, says it is no law, but a lewd custom. A governor is to conform himself to the laws of his own country, to the stipulations of those that employ him, and not to the lewd customs of any other country: those customs are more honored in the breach than in the observance."[64] The requirements of justice could be opposed to the dictates of public opinion. In his Bristol speech of 1780 Burke admitted that the public opposed measures of Catholic relief. But however general and deliberate that opposition was, it could claim no merit in justice. "When we know that the opinions of even the greatest multitudes are the standard of rectitude, I shall think myself obliged to make those opinions the master of my conscience." He acknowledged an obligation to make government pleasing to the people. "But the widest range of this politic complaisance is confined within the limits of justice."[65] In the end the right of the people to be respected in their historic peculiarities owed little to the status of those peculiarities as moral commandments. A custom or a prejudice might reflect latent wisdom; it might be an aid to morals; it might be an habitual virtue. But even if it were nothing more than an idle whim or fancy without moral significance, it still deserved the consideration and indulgence of the state. The people, Burke argued, had a claim to be gratified in their humours. "We are all a sort of children that must be soothed and managed. . . . I would bear, I would even myself play my part in, any innocent buffooneries, to divert them."[66] The basis of this claim lay not in any theory of historical jurisprudence, but in his conception of the state as a trust. As a trust, the state had an obligation to serve the happiness of its citizens. Men felt happiness and misery in their second natures; and to this extent government assumed a duty to consider the opinions, prejudices, and habits of its citizens.

The object of the state is (as far as may be) the happiness of the whole. Whatever makes multitudes of men utterly miserable can never answer that object;

[63] Burke, *Correspondence*, 2: 282.

[64] Burke, *Impeachment Speech on the Sixth Article*, in *Works*, 10: 268.

[65] Burke, *Speech upon Certain Points Relative to his Parliamentary Conduct*, in *Works*, 2: 421; *Correspondence*, 4: 274.

[66] Burke, *Speech upon Certain Points Relative to his Parliamentary Conduct*, in *Works*, 2: 421.

indeed, it contradicts it wholly and entirely; and the happiness or misery of mankind, estimated by their feelings and sentiments, and not by any theories of their rights, is, and ought to be, the standard for the conduct of legislators towards the people. This naturally and necessarily conducts us to the peculiar and characteristic situation of a people, and to a knowledge of their opinions, prejudices, habits, and all the circumstances that diversify and color life.[67]

The historical peculiarities of a people formed a proper object for the sovereign's solicitude. Presumably any policy or law which needlessly offended the people in their second natures could be condemned as a breach of equity. "It is not consistent with equity or wisdom to set at defiance the general feelings of great communities, and of all the orders which compose them."[68] It violated equity not because custom, prejudice, and opinion in themselves reflected the dictates of justice. It violated equity because the trustee bore a responsibility to make his subjects happy. "For as all government was originally instituted for the ease and benefit of the people, no establishment, which gives them nothing but uneasiness, can be approved by a wise legislature."[69] Whatever security the people enjoy in their historic peculiarities, it arises because Burke's sovereign is obliged by the principles of equity and justice. It does not arise because those peculiarities were assumed to reflect justice and equity.

[67] Burke, *Speech on the Unitarian Petition*, in *Works*, 7: 45.
[68] Burke, *Address to the King*, in *Works*, 6: 165.
[69] Burke, *Speeches*, 1: 61.

Six

Conclusion

Burke never expressly stated that he was the adherent of a particular political theory. On occasions he could cite the opinions of Montesquieu, Aristotle, and others to support himself in argument. These citations could be made in reverent and respectful terms: Aristotle was "the great master of reasoning"; Montesquieu was "a genius not born in every country or every time."[1] But these statements of admiration cannot be interpreted as confessions of discipleship. The closest Burke ever came to making an express commitment to the principles of other men was in the *Appeal*. Here he made his great profession of Whig orthodoxy. His principles, he claimed, were the same principles asserted by the Whigs of the Glorious Revolution.[2] "What these old Whigs pretended to be Mr. Burke is. This is enough for him."[3] Elsewhere, he boasted that the orthodoxy of his Whiggism had been demonstrated "beyond a possibility of debate."[4] This assertion of orthodoxy, if taken seriously, creates problems for the interpretation of Burke as an original and distinctive political theorist. A man who claims to believe what the old Whigs believed has disclaimed inventiveness and eccentricity. A man who associates himself with the Somerses, the Godolphins, and the Jekylls,[5] is not acknowledging a debt to Aristotle

[1] Burke, *Speech on Conciliation*, in *Works*, 2: 170; *Appeal*, in *Works*, 4: 211.
[2] Burke, *Appeal*, in *Works*, 4: 117-18, 148.
[3] Ibid., 149.
[4] Burke, *Correspondence*, 9: 446.
[5] Ibid., 6: 331.

and Montesquieu. He has asserted a kind of commitment that brings him suspiciously close to the principles of Lockean politics. Of course, an affirmation of Whig orthodoxy does not prove Lockean orthodoxy. Burke may not have believed the affirmation that he had made. He may have thought that the true principles of old Whiggism were quite different from the principles argued in Locke's *Treatises*. It is significant that when Burke expounded old Whiggism in the *Appeal* he did not cite Locke. He took as his authorities the Whigs who had conducted the impeachment of Dr. Sacheverell. Nevertheless, the fact remains that in the one statement Burke made on the source of his principles, he claimed an affiliation that contradicts many interpretations of his theory. It is not an affiliation that contradicts a Lockean interpretation.

No doubt, there are many ways in which it could be argued that Locke and Burke are different. In ethical theory Locke was a Rationalist; Burke was a Sentimentalist. Locke exhibits a bias towards democracy; Burke's bias is towards aristocracy. Burke recognized the variety of men; Locke implied their identity. Burke emphasized prudence; Locke emphasized rights. Locke was a formal philosopher who wrote treatises; Burke was a man of affairs who wrote pamphlets. Locke's *Treatises* were published to justify a revolution; Burke wrote his *Reflections* to condemn a revolution. If it is at all profitable to classify men as conservatives and liberals, there is a sense in which Burke is conservative and Locke is liberal. These and other distinctions can be asserted and possibly admitted. But in basic political theory, Burke adhered to a Lockean framework. He consistently respected two propositions that were crucial to Lockean politics. The first was that the state is an artificial institution which man has made by virtue of a legal engagement. The second was that the authority of the state is limited by the dictates of natural justice. When Locke argued for limited government, there were two theories of absolutism that had to be met: one formulated by Filmer and the other by Hobbes. Against Hobbes, Locke postulated the authority of natural justice. Against Filmer, he postulated the compact origins of the state. Neither of these postulates is violated in Burke's writings. Whether he argues for revolution or against revolution; whether he defends the state against the citizen or the citizen against the state, Burke's case ultimately rests on Lockean foundations. In this respect, Burke was the true Whig that he pretended to be and belongs in the end to the Lockean tradition of natural-rights individualism.

In his exposition of natural-rights individualism Burke sometimes departs from strict Lockean orthodoxy. It is possible that Locke either by intention or by inadvertence committed himself to a doctrine of majority rule. Burke did not. The democratic implication in natural-rights theory was something that Burke generally resisted. Secondly there is nothing in Locke that can explain Burke's appeal to prudential considerations. If Locke had returned from the grave to pronounce on the American controversy, there is no doubt that he would have sided with the Chathamites and the colonists in opposition to Burke. Property for Locke was a natural right; any effort to raise taxes without the consent of the tax-payer constituted a breach of this right. On this point the *Second Treatise* had been explicit and unmistakable.[6] Burke, as we have seen, disputed the natural-right argument and put the question in prudential terms. Where the levy of taxes was advantageous to the citizen, he could on Burke's account be taxed without his consent. But these differences between Burke and Locke do not arise from a collision of their fundamental premises. They arise, rather, from a disagreement on what might be considered a secondary level of speculation and argument. Both regarded government as a legal institution, but they did not agree in their definitions of its legal identity. Like Burke, Locke wrote of the state as if it were both a trust and a corporation. It is possible (though by no means certain) that Locke's conception of the state was coherent in a way that Burke's was not. If we hold Burke to all of his statements about trust and corporation, we are forced to suppose that the citizen is both a beneficiary and a corporator with respect to the same civil relationships. But one can read Locke on the supposition that natural men form civil society, which is a corporation, and that this corporation in turn settles authority on the legislative, which is a trustee.[7] On this understanding Burke's absurdity is avoided. Locke's citizen can be a member of a corporation; and the corporation that he belongs to can be regarded as the settlor and beneficiary of the trust. But whether Burke is more or less coherent than Locke in his conception of the state does not concern us here. The important point of difference is that in their respective conceptions of the trust and the corporation, Locke and Burke do not mean exactly the same kind of trust or exactly the same kind of corporation.

Locke's state, insofar as it may be interpreted as a corporation, has the power to act by a simple majority of its members. Once natural man is incorporated into civil society, the will of the majority signifies the will of all.[8] Civil society as a body politic may authorize the institution of a formal government. But the constitution of the formal government is not the constitution of civil society. For Locke, the formal government can lapse or forfeit its authority without dissolving the corporation that instituted it. A democratic corporation endures; it possesses the capacity to set up a new government; and if it chooses, it may set up a new

[6] Locke, *The Second Treatise of Civil Government and a Letter Concerning Toleration*, p. 71.

[7] Ibid., p. 119.

[8] Ibid., pp. 48-49.

government under a different form.[9] In Locke's state, the people, as distinct from their formal government, possess a corporate capacity that allows them to take collective action by the decision of a majority. When Burke talked about the state as a corporation, he assumed no distinction between the constitution of the people and the constitution of the government. The terms of incorporation that instituted the people in their collective capacity also instituted the form of their government. The select bodies that made up the formal government were the only representatives through which the corporate will of the people could be legally stated. Burke's citizens as corporators had no collective identity or coercive authority that was independent of their formal government. The French, Burke said, talked of the English nation: "we knew of no nation as a distinct body from the representative powers."[10] If the formal government failed or forfeited its right, there was for Burke no underlying corporation that allowed the people to express their collective will by majority vote. Locke could argue the right of a majority to act for the whole even if the constitution of the formal state were undemocratic. Burke could argue that majorities had no right to voice the corporate will unless that right were expressly specified in the formal constitution of the state:

> As in the abstract it is perfectly clear, that, out of a state of civil society, majority and minority are relations which can have no existence, and that, in civil society, its own specific conventions in each corporation determine what it is that constitutes the people, so as to make their act the signification of the general will,—to come to particulars, it is equally clear that neither in France nor in England has the original or any subsequent compact of the state, expressed or implied, constituted *a majority of men, told by the head*, to be the acting people of their several communities.[11]

The issue that divides Burke and Locke in their conception of the state as a corporate body is whether the power of action extends to the corporation at large or is confined to a select body. Both conceptions are intelligible in English law: some corporations are subject to the democratic government of their members; others are subject to the government of select bodies from which the members at large are excluded.[12] The question depends in the end on what one imagines to be the terms and conditions under which the corporation was originally created. Neither conception of state rules out absolutely the possibility of a revolution. Locke's conception, nevertheless, facilitates revolution in a way that Burke's does not. Locke's citizens can depose a govern-

[9] Ibid., pp. 119-20.

[10] Burke, *Speeches*, 4: 93.

[11] Burke, *Appeal*, in *Works*, 4: 173-74.

[12] Steward Kyd, *Treatise on the Law of Corporations*, 2 vols. (London: J. Butterworth, 1793-94), 1: 308.

ment and retain sufficient collective authority to establish a new one. Burke's citizens may depose a government, but in doing so they put their corporate capacity at risk. In a Burkean revolution that destroys the constitution of government, each corporator reverts to nature; the formation of a new constitution requires the formation of a new corporation; at this point Burke can insist that the new regime prove that its incorporation was consented to by all the subjects it claims as members.

In their respective conceptions of a trust, the difference between Locke and Burke is equally important. Burke's trust is a lawyer-like institution that corresponds to the trust of English equity. It is settled by the citizen and is administered for his benefit. But the trustee does not hold his authority at the pleasure of the citizen; nor is he accountable to the citizen's arbitrary judgment. The sovereign as trustee has equitable duties which he must discharge; the people as beneficiaries have equitable rights which can be enforced; but in the end the sovereign possesses a legal title to his authority which can be enforced against the will of the people. He is not a servant or an agent and on any charge of wrong-doing he has the right to be tried by standards of objective justice. In any dispute over the trustee's merits, the people in Burke's scheme figure not as judges but as suitors. As suitors they may possess a right to justice; but they do not possess a right to prescribe what justice is. "It is . . . of infinite importance that they should not be suffered to imagine that their will, any more than that of kings, is the standard of right and wrong."[13] On this conception of the trust Burke could argue that the government had the right and the duty to resist the demands of the people. Just as the trustee in English equity might be obliged to act against the wishes of the beneficiaries, so the sovereign as trustee could be obliged in justice to defy the popular will. "The body of the community, whenever it can come to act, can meet with no effectual resistance; but till power and right are the same, the whole body of them has no right inconsistent with virtue, and the first of all virtues, prudence. Men have no right to what is not reasonable, and to what is not for their benefit. . . ."[14] Burke's trust, in short, deprives the people of all political power or artificial authority. They are left with rights as the objects of the sovereign's benevolence, but they retain no right to dictate arbitrarily how that benevolence is to be exercised. The trust, furthermore, allows Burke to introduce utilitarian considerations into his argument. Whatever authority the government is deemed to possess in trust is held for the benefit and advantage of the citizen. To this extent, the citizen has a claim upon the trustee's wisdom and prudence. In contrast to Locke, Burke can assign to the government an indefinite jurisdiction. He can suppose when it suits him that the government has a right

[13] Burke, *Reflections*, in *Works*, 3: 355.
[14] Ibid., 313.

to levy taxes without the citizen's consent. He can suppose that different measures are due to different people in different circumstances. Yet in the end the exercise of the powers that belong to the trustee is still subject to the supervision of equity and justice.

If we read Locke in the most democratic sense of the text, his conception of a trust is much closer to an agency or deputation than to the trust of English law. His citizens transfer public authority into the care of a formal government. But they retain the right to revoke that authority if they decide that the trust has been abused. Locke's trustees, it might be argued, do not possess a legal title to their authority which may be asserted against the judgment of the settlor. To the question of who shall determine whether the trust has been honoured, Locke gave a democratic answer: "The people shall be judge; for who shall be judge whether the trustee or deputy acts well and according to the trust reposed in him, but he who deputes him, and must by having deputed him, have still the power to discard him when he fails in his trust? If this be reasonable in particular cases of private men, why should it be otherwise in that of the greatest moment, where the welfare of millions is concerned? . . ."[15] Whatever Locke's institution may be at this point, it is clearly something other than a trust as it is conceived in English law. First, the right of action under a trust belongs not to the settlor but to the beneficiary.[16] Secondly, the right of judgment belongs to neither, but to the Lord Chancellor. Locke does, of course, acknowledge that the jurisdiction of heaven lies beyond the jurisdiction of the people;[17] it is not impossible that he expected the people to be judges in good conscience and to try their trustees by some standard of justice. Nevertheless, the letter of Locke's argument bears a democratic implication. And it is easy to see why Burke made his appeal to the old Whigs in general and not to John Locke in particular.

To explain Burke's theory in Lockean terms requires us to run against the grain of conventional scholarship. With the exception of Walter D. Love and Burleigh T. Wilkins,[18] most students of Burke's theory find in it a fundamental and deliberate rejection of the principles of Lockean politics. It is not intended here to discuss every possible interpretation of Burke; there are three, however, that merit particular attention. The first identifies Burke as a common-law traditionalist; the

[15] Locke, *The Second Treatise of Civil Government and a Letter Concerning Toleration*, pp. 118-19.

[16] Maitland, "The Unincorporated Body," *Selected Essays*, pp. 121-32.

[17] Locke, *The Second Treatise of Civil Government and a Letter Concerning Toleration*, p. 119.

[18] Walter D. Love, "Edmund Burke's Idea of the Body Corporate: A Study in Imagery," *Review of Politics* 27 (1965): 184-97; "'Meaning' in the History of Conflicting Interpretations of Burke," *Burke Newsletter* 7 (1965-66): 526-38; Wilkins, *The Problem of Burke's Political Philosophy*.

second, as an organicist; the third, as a Thomist. Each of these interpretations in different ways divorces Burke from Locke and places Burke in opposition to the contract and natural-law theories that Locke typifies.

The analysis of Burke as a common-law traditionalist is the most recent of the three interpretations. It is entirely the work of J. G. A. Pocock.[19] Pocock argues that Burke in part was the heir of the common-law jurists of the seventeenth century; there is a similarity between Burke's conception of right and the conception of right found in the writings of Edward Coke and Matthew Hale. On Pocock's account Burke is a traditionalist not merely in the sense that he is psychologically disposed to favour old laws and old institutions; he is a traditionalist in the sense that the antiquity of a law or an institution supplies in itself evidence of its authority and rightness. "There was," for Pocock's Burke, ". . . always more in laws and institutions than met the eye of critical reason, always a case for them undiminished by anything that could be said against them." This theory of politics is "in a fairly obvious sense anti-rationalist"; it supposes that society possesses "an inner-life of growth and adaptation" which individual reason cannot entirely comprehend. According to Pocock, "Burke's thought can . . . properly be set in opposition to any rationalist system of politics, which presents political society as based originally on the assent of individual minds to universal principles rationally discerned."[20]

Pocock's study is primarily concerned with the sources and antecedents of Burke's jurisprudence. Much can be admitted in its favour. Pocock proves that a theory of common-law traditionalism developed in the seventeenth century; he shows that its influence persisted into the eighteenth century; he shows that Burke was familiar with the theory; he explains why Burke might appeal to immemorial law as a basis of authority in debate. What he does not prove, however, is that Burke ever endorsed this theory of jurisprudence or that Burke ever in fact argued that the antiquity of an historic law provided it with an authority in right. The evidence that is offered on this point is not conclusive; it suggests a more limited and hesitant acknowledgment of historic law than Pocock supposes.[21] Moreover, much evidence exists which shows that Burke either rejected mere legal tradition as a source of right or subordinated the authority of that tradition to the rational discretion of the political sovereign. Burke, as Pocock has reminded us, showed scant respect in his early years for the common-law interpretation of English history. He denied that Saxon law and the Saxon constitution were identical with the modern law and the modern con-

[19] Pocock, "Burke and the Ancient Constitution," pp. 125-43.
[20] Ibid., 125-26.
[21] See Appendix for detailed discussion of Pocock's proofs.

stitution.[22] He attacked Matthew Hale as an historian of English law and condemned common-law jurisprudence. "Thus the law has been confined and drawn up into a narrow and inglorious study. . . ." In the hands of the common-lawyers, the explanation of law had been dominated by "a species of reasoning" that was "the very refuse of the schools." These men had "deduced the spirit of the law, not from original justice or legal conformity, but from causes foreign to it and altogether whimsical."[23] There is little reason to think that Burke ever changed his mind in this matter. It is doubtful that common-law traditionalism explains his theory either in its entirety or in any part.

Whatever authority common law or historic law possessed for Burke, it did not supersede the discretion of Parliament. The latter had rights and duties that transcended historic law. This he argued in the *Sheriffs of Bristol*: American prisoners should not be tried as traitors, merely because they were traitors under formal law.

> Lawyers, I know, cannot make the distinction for which I contend; because they have their strict rule to go by. But legislators ought to do what lawyers cannot; for they have no other rules to bind them but the great principles of reason and equity and the general sense of mankind. These they are bound to obey and follow, and rather to enlarge and enlighten law by the liberality of legislative reason than to fetter and bind their higher capacity by the narrow constructions of subordinate, artificial justice.[24]

Burke made the identical point with reference to the historic rules and precedents that governed the procedure of the House of Commons. Again he contrasted the claims of formal and natural justice and gave his preference to the latter. "He was as much for a strict observance of the precedents of the House as any gentleman could be, as long as they were supported by reason; but technical rules should be done away whenever they were contrary to justice."[25]

Burke did not conceive of historic law in any sense as a set of self-validating rules. He might sometimes speak of a law as if it provided a presumptive proof of its utility. But the presumption of utility was neither absolute nor conclusive. When it suited his case, the presumption could be challenged and defeated. "A matter might be lawful," he reminded Lord North, "but not, therefore, expedient. There was a material distinction."[26]Burke admitted that the King possessed a legal right to dissolve Parliament. The exercise of the prerogative was "*prima facie* a right thing." ". . . But there might be circumstances . . . ," he continued, "which might prove, that what was *prima facie* right, was

[22] Burke, *Abridgment of English History*, in *Works*, 7: 312, 478.

[23] Ibid., 477.

[24] Burke, *Sheriffs of Bristol*, in *Works*, 2: 196-97.

[25] Burke, *Speeches*, 3: 262-63.

[26] Ibid., 2: 311.

altogether unjustifiable, and a most violent and unwarrantable exercise of power as ever was put in practice."[27] Moreover, he could imagine that an historic law lacked any merit in utility either present or past. In the debate on ex-officio information, it was his opponents and not Burke who equated old law with proven utility. Burke denied the equation. It was conceivable that the ex-officio information had injured the state. "Arguments enough have been already advanced to prove it unconstitutional and incompatible with liberty. What can be clearer evidence of its having never benefited the kingdom? The same arguments which prove it now prejudicial, prove it prejudicial ever since its commencement."[28] In the debate on the navy estimates of 1772, Burke again dismissed a defence that his opponents had made on the authority of ancient usage.

How weak an argument prescription is in this case, they do not seem to feel .... *Stare super vias antiquas* is their political creed. What then! is this maxim to preclude every improvement, however obvious and necessary, in the constitution? The first enquiry, before we proceed to walk upon this old road is, whether we can be said *star bene*, and the next is, whether, if this be the case, we cannot *star meglio*. If the latter part of the alternative is beyond our reach, then *sto qui* becomes a necessary, as well as prudential conclusion.[29]

Burke's distaste for the formalism of common law and his disregard for the claims of antiquity find their strongest expression in the impeachment speeches. Here, as we have seen, he subordinated the rules of common law to the requirements of natural justice and natural understanding. Hastings was to be tried not "upon the niceties of a narrow jurisprudence" but "upon the enlarged and solid principles of state morality."[30] He claimed that in the impeachment the Commons possessed the right to ignore the "common municipal law" and to disregard its forms. Parliament was not bound by traditional or historic rules of evidence. The managers could impeach Hastings "merely from the facts which were before them, upon the evident principles of common sense."[31] In the course of the trial, he argued that it was the duty of the Commons and the Lords to regulate the artificial justice of the common-law courts by the standards of natural justice.

As the privilege of impeachment was intended for the security of law and liberty, it was necessary that it should not be straightened in its mode of operation. They would have betrayed liberty, the constitution, and law, and justice itself, if they did not contend for a law of parliament, distinct from the law of Westminster-hall, paramount to it, and capable of superseding and

[27] Ibid., 3: 7.
[28] Ibid., 1: 60-61.
[29] Ibid., 1: 140.
[30] Burke, *Impeachment Speech in Opening*, in *Works*, 9: 333.
[31] Burke, *Speeches*, 3: 536.

controlling it in everything different from substantial justice. This he held to be so essential, that if, instead of the time that had been spent in its assertion, they had spent their whole lives in maintaining it, the time would have been well bestowed.[32]

Admittedly, Burke's case against the common-law rules of evidence was itself based in part upon an appeal to the authority of precedent and historic law. In contending for the law of Parliament against the common law, he opposed one set of historic rules against another set of historic rules. It is as if he argued for an historic and artificial privilege to plead the principles of natural justice and natural understanding. Burke never lost an argument by understating its merits. However, it is clear that his claim for natural justice went far beyond the historic privileges that he alleged for the law of Parliament. Common-sense rules of evidence were not only binding in this trial but in the trial of any criminal case. "The presumptions which belong to criminal cases are those natural and popular presumptions which are only observations turned into maxims. . . ."[33] In his efforts to show that his rules of evidence were endorsed by the latest and the best of the common-law judges, Burke almost represented the common law itself as a system that prescribed natural justice on the principles of natural reason.[34] "Such is the genius of the law of England," Burke contended, "that these two principles, of the general moral necessities of things, and the nature of the case, overrule every other principle, even those rules which seem the very strongest."[35] The derivative and subordinate characteristics of historic law were again asserted by Burke in reply to Hastings' defence that the precedents of the East justified his conduct. "There is but one law for all," Burke responded, "namely, that law which governs all law, the law of our Creator, the law of humanity, justice, equity,—the Law of Nature and of Nations. So far as any laws fortify this primeval law, and give it more precision, more energy, more effect by their declarations, such laws enter into the sanctuary, and participate in the sacredness of its character."[36] Whatever authority historical law possessed for Burke, that authority was derived from a conception of justice that owed nothing to the force of precedent or to the claims of antiquity.

It is true that Burke often professed a reverence for the historic constitution. But it is unlikely that the authority of his constitution owed anything to the authority of simple tradition. When he wrote of the state as a trust, he supposed that it had the right to alter the

[32] Ibid., 3: 537-38.

[33] Burke, *Report from the Committee Appointed to Inspect the Lords' Journals*, in *Works*, 11: 94.

[34] See Burke's citations of Lord Chief-Justices Lee and Mansfield in ibid., 83-84.

[35] Ibid., 82.

[36] Burke, *Impeachment Speech in Reply*, in *Works*, 11: 225.

constitution as circumstances required. The constitution had been changed in the past and might be changed again in the future. Presumably, the merit of the constitution lay in its utility and its forms were liable to alteration at the judgment of the trustee. When he wrote of the state as a corporation, this discretion was denied. It was not denied, however, on the assumption that ancient usage creates right. The authority of the corporate constitution was based on the authority of compact. History and prescription might conceivably teach men what the terms of their compact were. "What the particular nature of that agreement was is collected from the form into which the particular society has been cast. Any other is not *their* covenant."[37] Here, Burke based his argument on an assumption that was neither traditionalist nor historicist in character. It was an assumption that he shared with Locke, and, for that matter, also shared with Hobbes. This is that men are bound by their engagements. To the extent that the constitution was a creature of men's promises, men were obliged to respect its terms. "The Constitution of a country being once settled upon some compact, tacit or expressed, there is no power existing of force to alter it, without breach of the covenant, or the consent of all the parties."[38] Burke might appeal to history to reveal the terms of civil obligation; he did not argue that history itself supplied those terms or that antiquity, however great, added anything to their authority.

The notion that Burke entertained an organic theory of society probably started with Leslie Stephen in the nineteenth century.[39] Stephen's interpretation no longer dominates the field. Modern scholars, however, continue to give it a measure of partial endorsement. Stanlis has written of Burke's "insistence that the state was a complex living organism which waxes to maturity through centuries." Whenever the state was in difficulties Burke, on Stanlis' account, fitted "his prescription for improvement to all that has contributed to its organic growth."[40] In more cautious terms, Wilkins has also argued for an element of organicism in Burke's social theory.[41] It would be unfair to suggest that either Wilkins or Stanlis sees organicism as central to his interpretation of Burke. Neither presses it to the extent that Stephen did. Nevertheless, in their partial admission of the organicist interpretation, both illustrate the force of Stephen's powerful but mistaken legacy. The case against the organicist interpretation has been fully stated by Walter D. Love.[42] The main objection is that Burke supplies

[37] Burke, *Appeal*, in *Works*, 4: 169-70.

[38] Ibid., 162.

[39] Love, "Conflicting Interpretations of Burke," p. 527.

[40] Stanlis, *Edmund Burke and the Natural Law*, p. 210.

[41] Wilkins, *The Problem of Burke's Political Philosophy*, pp. 114, 218.

[42] Love, "Idea of the Body Corporate," pp. 184-97; "Conflicting Interpretations of Burke," pp. 526-38.

us with no explicit evidence which proves that he seriously thought the state resembled an organism. As Love has shown us, the explicit evidence suggests that Burke denied all resemblance between the two. "These analogies between bodies natural and politic," wrote Burke in the *Letter to William Elliot*, "though they may sometimes illustrate arguments, furnish no argument of themselves."[43] Again in the *Regicide Peace*: "Parallels of this sort rather furnish similitudes to illustrate or to adorn than to supply analogies from whence to reason." Natural and political bodies did not belong to "the same classes of existence." The state was an artificial body, a moral essence; it was not a physical body; nor did it hold any "assignable connection" with the physical order.[44] Admittedly, Burke did use organic language from time to time. He could write of the state and its institutions in biological terms; he could use figures that implied growth and development. There is no reason to think, however, that in doing so he intended or assumed any meaning in these statements beyond the figurative and metaphorical. On the evidence of Burke's own remarks we can dismiss his organicist figures as ornaments to an argument that itself owed nothing to organicist assumptions.

The organicist interpretation of Burke was never grounded on conclusive evidence. Whatever merit it possessed depended primarily on its value as an hypothesis that accounted for Burke's theories of historical change and social cohesion. This study has tried to show that we can account for both without resorting to organicist assumptions. Burke's theory of natural society and his theory of human nature can be explained entirely in terms of individualistic psychology. Burke's natural men live together in a group, not because the group possesses an organic identity, but because each member of the group is endowed with social impulses. To call Burke's natural society an organicist conception adds no more to our understanding of it than it would to call Adam Smith's marketplace an organicist conception. The changes that Burke describes in human nature and in natural society were not changes that violated the orthodoxies of eighteenth-century individualism. Through force of association natural men acquired distinctive habits and customs; through force of individual imitation and admiration these distinctive peculiarities could be transmitted to other members of the society. To explain this kind of change, we do not need to suppose that man's nature developed organically; nor do we need to suppose that Burke endowed the natural community with an animus or vitality that was distinct from the animus and vitality of its individual members. Burke assumed no principles of social change and development that were not principles of individual change and development.

[43] Burke, *A Letter to William Elliot . . .* , in *Works*, 5: 124.

[44] Burke, *Regicide Peace*, in *Works*, 5: 234.

His conception of civil society on the other hand was thoroughly juridical. Whatever political changes he countenanced or condemned, the basis of his argument rested upon law and legal obligation. When he wished to alter the constitution or applaud an alteration that had been made in the past, he invoked the discretionary duty of the trustee. When he wished to prohibit or condemn a change, as he did in the French Revolution, he invoked the authority of the original compact. In short organicism explains nothing in Burke that cannot be explained upon more plausible and evident principles. It rests upon no explicit evidence; it solves no problems; and it creates immense difficulties for the interpretation of Burke as a consistent thinker.

The argument that Burke's political theory is in some significant sense Thomistic has been the work of many scholars. Leo Strauss, Peter Stanlis, and Francis Canavan may be singled out as its representative exponents. On Stanlis' interpretation, Burke was "essentially a Thomist in his political philosophy."[45] On Strauss's, Burke is said to have integrated his notions of natural right "into a classical or Thomistic framework."[46] For Canavan: "The basic premises of Burke's mature political thought . . . strongly resemble those of medieval Christian Aristotelianism."[47] If the Thomistic interpretation of Burke means simply that Burke asserted the authority of natural justice, there can be no objection to it. If Burke is thought to be a Thomist in the same sense in which Locke might be described as a Thomist, the interpretation is valid. It rests upon explicit evidence; it illuminates Burke's arguments in a way that alternative explanations do not; it is moreover an interpretation of Burke to which this present study is much indebted. But if the emphasis on Burke's Thomism bears the meaning that Burke rejected Lockean politics and argued natural-law principles in an old-fashioned and an eccentric sense, then it is demonstrably wrong. As we have seen Burke asserted natural-law principles in a manner that was fully consistent with Lockean individualism. Throughout his life he consistently assumed the bases of Lockean theory. He assumed the priority of natural law over the positive law of the state. He assumed that the citizen possessed rights that could be asserted against the state. He accepted the reality of natural society. And perhaps most important of all, he accepted the Lockean premise that the state was the creature of artificial compact.

The objection to the Thomist interpretation, and, for that matter, to any interpretation that divorces Burke from Locke, is twofold. First, it tends to make Burke somewhat implausible as a politician. As long as Burke's theory is explained in terms that his contemporaries under-

[45] Stanlis, *Edmund Burke and the Natural Law*, p. 249.

[46] Strauss, *Natural Right and History*, p. 296.

[47] Canavan, *The Political Reason of Edmund Burke*, p. 205.

stand and acknowledge, we can study Burke as a theorist without disregarding the probabilities of his public career. As a politician and a man of affairs, Burke was presumably inspired to adopt policies for a variety of reasons, reasons that perhaps had little to do with doctrine or philosophy. His defence of those policies in debate may well suppose a political theory that is more or less coherent; but it is likely to be a political theory that his audience understands and endorses. Lockean theory for Burke is not an encumbrance in public life. We can interpret Burke as a Lockean without having to imagine that he was liable to some special kind of doctrinal inspiration or that he chose to defend his policy in anachronistic terms. However, once we begin to interpret Burke in terms of an eccentric and unorthodox political theory, he begins to look less like a politician answerable to the realities of public life and more like a closet-philosopher or a doctrinaire. Of course, this does not prove that Burke was not a closet-philosopher or a doctrinaire. He may in the end have been either. But in terms of political biography a Burke who talks like Locke is much easier to understand than a Burke who talks like St. Thomas. The second objection is perhaps more serious. Both Canavan and Strauss acknowledge that Burke sometimes argued on Lockean premises. Neither is disposed to admit such arguments as evidence in his exposition of Burke's principles. The Thomism which they find in Burke is really a secret or semi-conscious doctrine that Burke is deemed to hold in defiance of his insincere or accidental professions of Lockeanism. Strauss's Burke is an artful man who often cadges votes on pretexts that he does not truly believe. Canavan's Burke is the innocent victim of Lockean terms and conceptions that had been devised to serve a political theory quite different from his own.[48] Of course, it would be naive to imagine that Burke always spoke from the heart; it would be unrealistic to deny that men sometimes invoke terms and conceptions whose full implication they might reject. The distinction that is drawn between the true Burke and the false Burke is not outrageous. But it fails in the end, because there is no way of demonstrating when Burke is speaking with sincerity or deliberation. If the Burke who talks like Locke is a false Burke, how then can we tell that the Burke who talks like St. Thomas is genuine and authentic? The only way that we can study Burke's theory is to adhere to the text of his argument. If that argument is explicitly Lockean in character, our interpretation of Burke must accommodate the evidence of his statement.

Our estimate of Burke's merit as a political theorist depends a great deal on the questions that we ask. If the question is whether Burke consistently argued a coherent set of principles, then his claims as a

[48] Strauss, *Natural Right and History*, p. 296; Canavan, *The Political Reason of Edmund Burke*, pp. 88, 114.

theorist cannot be disputed. Throughout his life Burke continued to assert the same principles. His most serious lapse from consistency occurs in his shift from trust to corporation. But this lapse does not contradict his general commitment to the compact theory of the state. Moreover, there are perhaps very few contractualists who are perfectly consistent in their conception of the legal institution which the citizen is supposed to create by virtue of his consent. If we allow Burke some indulgence on the grounds that he was not a philosopher writing a treatise but a debater arguing different cases at different times, then the degree of consistency he exhibits in his arguments is impressive. Furthermore, there is little reason to think that Burke developed or matured in the basic principles of his theory. It is possible that his attitudes and opinions changed over time. As he grew older he may have become more conservative and less democratic in his preferences. Yet there is no strong evidence of development in his bases of argument. In the 1790s as in the 1760s Burke continued to appeal to the same standards of authority: to natural justice, to human nature and natural society, and to the terms of civil compact. As a politician, Burke, very possibly, had neither the time nor the inclination to think creatively about abstract political theory. The theory that he had mastered in his youth and brought with him into public life remained with him unchanged until his death.

If our estimate of Burke as a theorist depends upon the question of his philosophical inspiration, then we pose a problem to which there is no answer. Burke's consistency of argument may in the end signify nothing more than consistency of pretext. We cannot assume that because he appealed to the same principles in controversy that those principles necessarily inspired him to adopt the policies and purposes that he defended. Nor can we assume the contrary. Because Burke's statements of philosophy served his controversial purpose, we cannot suppose that the philosophy was simply affected for the occasion. There are no conclusive proofs for sincerity. But it is worth remembering that Burke never squandered his philosophy. There is always a very intimate connection between his statements of theory and his political objective. His appeals to principle were generally calculated to advance his argument. He may or may not have believed in the authority of natural justice; in the Hastings impeachment, however, he had little choice but to assert natural justice against the claims of positive law. He may or may not have believed that the state owed prudential obligations to its citizens; but in the American controversy, this assumption allowed him to oppose taxation and at the same time to adhere to the principles of the Declaratory Act. He may or may not have come to believe that the state was a corporation, yet this assumption allowed him to condemn the National Assembly and to defend the pretensions of the *émigrés*. Burke's statements of theory can never be divorced from the controversial context in which they were made. Whatever we may think about Burke's sincerity or the extent of his philosophical inspiration, Burke's political theory was not a useless or quixotic system. He talked to his contemporaries in language that they understood and claimed their support on principles that they could hardly disavow. There is no need to imagine that Burke stated his arguments for the benefit of posterity or that he undertook to convert his contemporaries to a new system of political truth.

If the question we ask is whether Burke made a major contribution to the development of political theory, the answer must be that he did not. He wrote and speculated within the framework of natural-rights individualism; there is nothing in the text of his writings to suggest that he rebelled against the orthodoxies of his time or that he anticipated the novelties of nineteenth-century speculation. To picture Burke as a profound and original thinker is to misread the principles that he actually asserted. It is moreover to thrust upon him a status which he laid no claim to. Like most politicians he pretended that his principles were the principles of all right-thinking men. When he defended the *Reflections* he denied his originality. He said that it had been his purpose to convey to the French, not his own ideas, but "the prevalent opinions and sentiments" of the people of England. "His representation is authenticated by the verdict of his country. Had his piece, as a work of skill, been thought worthy of commendation, some doubt might have been entertained of the cause of his success. But the matter stands exactly as he wishes it."[49] Here and throughout the 1790s the last thing that Burke wanted to possess was a reputation for inventiveness. What he laid claim to was the merit of consistency and orthodoxy. As a political theorist, Burke's strength did not lie in originality. What he displayed, rather, was a brilliant dexterity in the manipulation of conventional truths. He took the Lockean assumptions of his age and applied them to the diverse occasions of public life. Perhaps his greatest achievement was to purge those assumptions of their revolutionary implications. For all practical purposes, the old Whig theory of politics had been developed to justify revolution. Throughout the eighteenth century it retained its revolutionary flavour and significance. Burke's great service lay not in discrediting or refuting those Lockean assumptions but in showing that they could be invoked in favour of the old regime. The principles of 1688 did not necessarily condemn the governments of 1789. Burke showed that the Lockean premises of his age could be worked to justify the institutions that he and his contemporaries wished to defend. After he had published the *Appeal* Burke received a letter of appreciation from Lord Camden. Camden was a

[49] Burke, *Appeal*, in *Works*, 4: 63-64.

Chathamite who had argued a strict Lockean line in opposition to Burke in the American controversy.[50] On this occasion he declared his "perfect concurrence" with Burke's doctrine. "I . . . like many others, have always thought myself an Old Whig, and held the same principles with yourself, but I suppose none or very few of us ever thought upon the subject with so much correctness, and hardly any would be able to express their . . . thoughts with such Clearness, justness and force of Argument."[51] This exemplifies the testimony that Burke had courted; it exemplifies the testimony that he deserved.

[50] J. W. Gough, *Fundamental Law in English Constitutional History* (Oxford: Clarendon Press, 1955), pp. 193-95.

[51] Burke, *Correspondence*, 6: 333, fn. 3.

Appendix

J. G. A. Pocock's argument that Burke acknowledged historic law as a source of right is based upon the evidence of two passages. The first appears in the *Reflections*. Quoted in part, it reads:

Our oldest reformation is that of Magna Charta. You will see that Sir Edward Coke, that great oracle of our law, and indeed all the great men who follow him, to Blackstone, are industrious to prove the pedigree of our liberties. They endeavour to prove that the ancient charter, the Magna Charta of King John, was connected with another positive charter from Henry the First, and that both the one and the other were nothing more than a reaffirmance of the still more ancient standing law of the kingdom. In the matter of fact, for the greater part, these authors appear to be in the right; perhaps not always: but if the lawyers mistake in some particulars, it proves my position still the more strongly; because it demonstrates the powerful prepossession towards antiquity with which the minds of all our lawyers and legislators, and of all the people whom they wish to influence, have been always filled, and the stationary policy of this kingdom in considering their most sacred rights and franchises as an *inheritance*.[1]

This passage perhaps proves that Burke recognized and understood the common-law tradition of the seventeenth century. However, it does not prove that he endorsed its truth, either as a theory of jurisprudence or as a theory of history. Burke quite explicitly avoided grounding his case upon the accuracy of the common-law interpretation. If the

[1] Burke, *Reflections*, in *Works*, 3: 272-73; quoted in Pocock, "Burke and the Ancient Constitution," p. 127.

lawyers were mistaken in some particulars, it proved his position all the more strongly. Presumably, it would not have mattered too much if they had been mistaken in all their particulars. What Burke chose to applaud was not the accuracy of their interpretation of law and history but the utility of their presumption as a matter of public policy. When he came to justify that policy later in the *Reflections*, it was not done on the grounds of its historical or jurisprudential merits; he justified the policy on the grounds that it conformed to nature. "This policy appears to me to be the result of profound reflection,—or rather the happy effect of following Nature, which is wisdom without reflection, and above it." He called it "a constitutional policy working after the pattern of Nature." It was a way of "preserving the method of Nature in the conduct of the state." Whatever historical basis of argument he may have assumed was cast aside. "By adhering . . . to our forefathers, we are guided not by the superstition of antiquarians, but by the spirit of philosophic analogy." In short what Burke defended in this passage of the *Reflections* is not the common-law tradition as an authority in right, but the common-law tradition as an expedient policy. "We procure reverence to our civil institutions on the principle upon which Nature teaches us to revere individual men: on account of their age, and on account of those from whom they are descended."[2] The merit of the common-law tradition rested in the end upon Burke's theory of human psychology and not on his theory of jurisprudence.

The second passage appears in the *Speech on Reform of the Representation*. Quoted in part, it reads:

> Our Constitution is a prescriptive constitution; it is a constitution whose sole authority is, that it has existed time out of mind. . . . Your king, your lords, your judges, your juries . . . all are prescriptive; and what proves it is the disputes, not yet concluded, and never near becoming so, when any of them first originated. Prescription is the most solid of all titles, not only to property, but, which is to secure that property, to government. . . . It is accompanied with another ground of authority in the constitution of the human mind, presumption. It is a presumption in favor of any settled scheme of government against any untried project, that a nation has long existed and flourished under it. It is a better presumption even of the *choice* of a nation,—far better than any sudden and temporary arrangement by actual election. . . . Nor is prescription of government formed upon blind, unmeaning prejudices. For man is a most unwise and a most wise being. The individual is foolish; the multitude, for the moment, is foolish, when they act without deliberation; but the species is wise, and, when time is given to it, as a species, it almost always acts right.[3]

Considered in isolation this passage confirms Pocock's interpretation. Burke here is arguing the authority of prescription, and arguing it

[2] Burke, *Reflections*, in *Works*, 3: 274-76.

[3] Burke, *Speech on Reform of the Representation*, in *Works*, 7: 94-95, quoted in Pocock, "Burke and the Ancient Constitution," p. 140.

with warmth and approbation. But in the context of the entire speech Burke's appeal to prescription is more guarded and limited than Pocock's reading suggests. Burke started the speech with an account of the case for electoral reform. It was based, he said, on two arguments that were "utterly irreconcilable." The first was an argument for personal representation. It supposed that man possessed a natural right to govern himself and that this right might be exercised through the office of a representative. Any form of government that violated this right was a usurpation and had no claim upon the obedience of the citizen. Burke's account of this argument tended to be indulgent. He said that it was "plain and intelligible."[4] Later in the speech he described it as the "only thing distinct and sensible that has been advocated."[5] Burke's account of the second argument is less easy to grasp. He said the second argument was political in character as opposed to the first that was juridical. The second argument rejected the right of personal representation with "scorn and fervor." The basis of the second argument, as far as Burke stated it, was that the existing system of representation was not framed to answer the theory of its institution.[6] Very possibly, Burke meant that the second argument appealed either to the original form of the constitution or to the principles upon which the original constitution was grounded.

At this stage of his speech, Burke began to talk prescription. One thing is evident. However partial Burke was to the constitution on its prescriptive basis, he did not contend that the appeal to prescription defeated the argument from natural right. "As to the first sort of reformers," he admitted, "it is ridiculous to talk to them of the British Constitution upon any or upon all of its bases. . . ."[7] Given the indulgent terms in which Burke first described their arguments, I do not think we can take Burke to mean that the natural-right reformers were too stubborn or bone-headed to understand an appeal to prescription. Burke's point seems to be that the argument from prescription did not meet the argument which they had advanced upon the claim of natural right. Burke's refutation of the natural-right argument occurs somewhat later in his speech. And it does not assert the authority of prescription. Meeting the argument of a natural-right opponent, Burke replied: "Now what does this go to, but to lead directly to anarchy? For to discredit the only government which he either possesses or can project, what is this but to destroy all government? and this is anarchy."[8] This objection, I think, anticipates the argument that he was later to use against the French revolutionaries. This argument is that the claim of a

[4] Burke, *Speech on Reform of the Representation*, in *Works*, 7: 92-93.
[5] Ibid., 102.
[6] Ibid., 92.
[7] Ibid., 93.
[8] Ibid., 102.

natural right to self-government worked not only against a particular kind of government but against all kinds of government. Man cannot claim under the conventions of civil society a right that supposes that civil society does not exist, "rights which are absolutely repugnant to it."[9]

Burke introduced the appeal to prescription to refute not the advocates of the first argument but the advocates of the second. The claim of natural right he showed worked not only against the Commons, as it was then constituted, but against the Crown and Lords as well. Those who would confine their reformation to the Commons had to resort to the argument of prescription to justify the authority of the King and the Lords. "Why, what have you to answer in favor of the prior rights of the crown and peerage but this. . . . "[10] Then follows the passage quoted by Pocock in which Burke asserts prescription as a source of right. Prescription gives a solid title to property and to government. It justifies a presumption of consent and a presumption of utility. He argues the point using terms of endorsement and commitment. Once the prescriptive title is stated, Burke goes on to demonstrate that the prescriptive claims of the Commons are just as good as the prescriptive claims of the King and the Lords. "Now if the crown, and the lords . . . are all prescriptive, so is the House of Commons of the very same origin."[11] He argued that the Commons remained what it had been at its original institution. It could not be assumed that the composition of the Commons violated the terms of its institution. "To ask whether a thing which has always been the same stands to its usual principle seems to me to be perfectly absurd: for how do you know the principles, but from the construction? and if that remains the same, the principles remain the same."[12] Burke proceeded to make the same point with reference to the whole constitution:

> A prescriptive government, such as ours, never was the work of any legislator, never was made upon any foregone theory. It seems to me a preposterous way of reasoning, and a perfect confusion of ideas, to take the theories which learned and speculative men have made from that government, and then, supposing it made on those theories which were made from it, to accuse the government as not corresponding with them.[13]

Burke's defence of the historic constitution is grounded upon prescription to this extent: against those who argued for constitutional reform on the supposition that the constitution had departed from its

[9] Burke, *Reflections*, in *Works*, 3: 309-10; *Appeal*, in *Works*, 4: 188; *The Conduct of the Minority*, in *Works*, 5: 45-46.

[10] Burke, *Speech on Reform of the Representation*, in *Works*, 7: 93-94.

[11] Ibid., 95.

[12] Ibid., 96, quoted in Pocock, "Burke and the Ancient Constitution," p. 141.

[13] Burke, *Speech on Reform of the Representation*, in *Works*, 7: 96-97, quoted in Pocock, "Burke and the Ancient Constitution," p. 141.

original terms or principles he invokes the authority of prescription. He replied in essence that the constitution was what it had always been, and that the only way you could discover its original principles was to study its present construction. Quite clearly, however, Burke admitted limits to the force of the prescriptive argument. It worked against those who supposed an original constitution and demanded reform of the present constitution to restore it to its original form. It did not work against all criticism and all demands for reform. "It is true that to say your Constitution is what it has been is no sufficient defence for those who say it is a bad constitution."[14] To meet this claim for reform, Burke introduced utilitarian considerations. "To those who say it is a bad one, I answer, Look to its effects. In all moral machinery, the moral results are its test."[15] Burke used prescription to argue the identity of the ancient and modern constitutions. When he came to assert the merit and authority of the historic constitution, he moved from prescription to utility. He supposed that anyone who rejected the argument from natural right was forced to follow his example. "If you reject personal representation, you are pushed upon expedience. . . ." "If the only specific plan proposed, individual personal representation, is directly rejected . . . then the only way of considering it is a question of convenience."[16] Burke argued that historical experience supplied evidence of utility. It was a better guide than mere speculation. "If we are to judge of a commonwealth actually existing, the first thing I inquire is, What has been *found* expedient or inexpedient?"[17] Whether Burke appealed to past or to present utility, he admitted a consideration that defeated his argument from prescription. He admitted a non-historical standard that made it difficult to defend the constitution on the grounds of its antiquity.

All in all, I do not think that this text proves Pocock's interpretation. Burke did argue from prescription. It is doubtful, however, that he asserted prescription against the claim of natural right. It is doubtful that he thought prescription supplied an absolute justification for the historic constitution. He used prescription against those who supposed the authority of a prior and more authentic constitution, but in the end he appealed to a standard of justification that could discredit the historic constitution and allow it to be changed or discarded. On the evidence of this speech, Burke's commitment to the ancient constitution and to the common-law tradition seems equivocal. On the evidence of his other works, there is much to suggest that Burke explicitly rejected the tradition in which Pocock has placed him.

[14] Burke, *Speech on Reform of the Representation*, in *Works*, 7: 96, quoted in Pocock "Burke and the Ancient Constitution," p. 141.

[15] Burke, *Speech on Reform of the Representation*, in *Works*, 7: 96.

[16] Ibid., 97, 102.

[17] Ibid., 98.

Bibliography

Burke, Edmund. *A Notebook of Edmund Burke*. Edited by H. V. F. Somerset. Cambridge: At the University Press, 1957.

———. *Extracts from Mr. Burke's Table-Talk Written Down by Mrs. Crewe*. London: Philobiblion Society, 1862.

———. *The Correspondence of Edmund Burke*. Edited by Thomas W. Copeland et al. 9 vols. to date. Cambridge: At the University Press; Chicago: University of Chicago Press, 1958-.

———. *The Speeches of . . . Edmund Burke . . . .* 4 vols. London: Longman, Hurst, Rees and Brown; and J. Ridgway, 1816.

———. *The Writings and Speeches of Edmund Burke*. 12 vols. Boston: Little, Brown and Co., 1901.

Canavan, Francis P. *The Political Reason of Edmund Burke*. Durham, N.C.: Duke University Press, 1960.

Cobban, Alfred. *Edmund Burke and the Revolt against the Eighteenth Century: A Study of the Political and Social Thinking of Burke, Wordsworth, Coleridge and Southey*. 2d ed. London: George Allen & Unwin, 1960.

Cone, Carl B. "Burke and the European Social Order." *Thought* 39 (1964): 273-88.

Courtney, C. P. *Montesquieu and Burke*. London: Basil Blackwell, 1963.

Dreyer, Frederick. "Burke's Religion." *Studies in Burke and His Time* 7 (1976): 199-212.

———. "The Genesis of Burke's *Reflections*." *Journal of Modern History* 50 (1978): 462-79.

Fennessy, R. R. *Burke, Paine and the Rights of Man: A Difference of Political Opinion*. The Hague: Martinus Nijhoff, 1963.

Gough, J. W. *Fundamental Law in English Constitutional History*. Oxford: Clarendon Press, 1955.

Grant, James. *A Practical Treatise on the Law of Corporations in General, as Well Aggregate as Sole*. London: Butterworth's, 1850.

Holdsworth, William. *A History of English Law*. 16 vols. 1938-66; reprint ed. London: Methuen & Co.; Sweet & Maxwell, 1966.

Hutchins, Robert M. "The Theory of Oligarchy: Edmund Burke." *Thomist* 5 (1943): 61-78.

__________. "The Theory of the State: Edmund Burke." *Review of Politics* 5 (1943): 139-55.

Keeton, George W. *The Law of Trusts: A Statement of the Rules of Law and Equity Applicable to Trusts of Real and Personal Property*. 9th ed. London: Pitman Publishing, 1971.

Kyd, Stewart. *Treatise on the Law of Corporations*. 2 vols. London: J. Butterworth, 1793-94.

Locke, John. *The Second Treatise of Civil Government and a Letter Concerning Toleration*. Edited by J. W. Gough. Rev. ed. Oxford: Basil Blackwell, 1948.

Love, Walter D. "Edmund Burke's Idea of the Body Corporate: A Study in Imagery." *Review of Politics* 27 (1965): 184-97.

__________. "'Meaning' in the History of Conflicting Interpretations of Burke." *Burke Newsletter* 7 (1965-66): 526-38.

Mahoney, Thomas H. D. *Edmund Burke and Ireland*. Cambridge, Mass.: Harvard University Press, 1960.

Maitland, Frederick W. *Selected Essays*. Edited by H. D. Hazeltine et al. 1936; reprint ed. Freeport, N.Y.: Books for Libraries Press, 1968.

Marshall, P. J. *The Impeachment of Warren Hastings*. Oxford: Oxford University Press, 1965.

Mill, James. *The History of British India*. 9 vols. London: J. Madden, 1840-48.

Morley, John. *Burke*. London: Macmillan & Co., 1907.

O'Gorman, Frank. *Edmund Burke: His Political Philosophy*. London: George Allen & Unwin, 1973.

Paine, Thomas. *The Political Works of Thomas Paine*. New York: Liberal and Scientific Publishing House, 1878.

Parkin, Charles. *The Moral Basis of Burke's Political Thought*. Cambridge: At the University Press, 1956.

Pocock, J. G. A. "Burke and the Ancient Constitution: A Problem in the History of Ideas." *Historical Journal* 3 (1960): 125-43.

Stanlis, Peter J. *Edmund Burke and the Natural Law*. Ann Arbor: University of Michigan Press, 1958.

Strauss, Leo. *Natural Right and History*. Chicago: University of Chicago Press, 1953.

Vattel, Emerich von. *The Law of Nations: Or Principles of the Law of Nature Applied to the Conduct and Affairs of Nations and Sovereigns*. Philadelphia: P. H. Nicklin and T. Johnson, 1829.

Wilkins, Burleigh T. *The Problem of Burke's Political Philosophy*. Oxford: Clarendon Press, 1967.

Index